Reading the Waves

Reading the Waves

A Memoir

LIDIA YUKNAVITCH

RIVERHEAD BOOKS

NEW YORK

2025

RIVERHEAD BOOKS
An imprint of Penguin Random House LLC
penguinrandomhouse.com

Copyright © 2025 by Lidia Yuknavitch
Penguin Random House values and supports copyright. Copyright
fuels creativity, encourages diverse voices, promotes free speech, and
creates a vibrant culture. Thank you for buying an authorized edition
of this book and for complying with copyright laws by not reproducing,
scanning, or distributing any part of it in any form without permission.
You are supporting writers and allowing Penguin Random House to
continue to publish books for every reader. Please note that no part of
this book may be used or reproduced in any manner for the purpose of
training artificial intelligence technologies or systems.

Riverhead and the R colophon are registered trademarks
of Penguin Random House LLC.

Some pieces of this storytelling have appeared in different forms in
BOMB, *The Rumpus*, and the anthology *The Lonely Stories* (Catapult,
2022). Smaller portions have appeared in different arrangements in the
novels *The Small Backs of Children* (Harper, 2015), *Thrust* (Riverhead,
2022), and *The Book of Joan* (Harper, 2017).

Book design by Amanda Dewey

LIBRARY OF CONGRESS CATALOGING-IN-PUBLICATION DATA

Names: Yuknavitch, Lidia, author.
Title: Reading the waves : a memoir / Lidia Yuknavitch.
Description: New York : Riverhead Books, 2024.
Identifiers: LCCN 2024035071 (print) | LCCN 2024035072 (ebook) |
ISBN 9780593713051 (hardcover) | ISBN 9780593713068 (ebook)
Subjects: LCSH: Yuknavitch, Lidia. |
Women authors, American—Oregon—Portland—Biography.
Classification: LCC PS3575.U35 Z46 2024 (print) |
LCC PS3575.U35 (ebook) | DDC 813/.6 [B]—dc23/eng/20241028
LC record available at https://lccn.loc.gov/2024035071
LC ebook record available at https://lccn.loc.gov/2024035072

Printed in the United States of America
1st Printing

Some names and identifying characteristics have been changed
to protect the privacy of the individuals involved.

For Devin.
And for all those who find themselves
suspended between the fall and the leap.

Contents

Reading yourself as a fiction as well as a fact is the only way to keep the narrative open—the only way to stop the story from running away under its own momentum, often towards an ending no one wants.

~ Jeanette Winterson,
Why Be Happy When You Could Be Normal?

When I think of what I already lived through it seems to me I was shedding my bodies along the paths.

~ Clarice Lispector, *Água Viva*

There is no such thing as repetition. Only insistence.

~ Gertrude Stein, *Lectures in America*

Arrange whatever pieces come your way.

~ Virginia Woolf, *A Writer's Diary*

Reading the Waves

Preface:
A Return

*T*his is not a hero's journey, or a traditional memoir, though travel and memory and storytelling are all in these pages. I do not intend to mine my personal life for dramatic scenes and serve them up. I mean to read a few episodes from my life not as facts but as fictions, as stories that lodged in my body. Is there a way to liberate them? To rearrange the elements narratively? Might I create a hermeneutics to my own memories? Memory is always a kind of return; I mean to make a series of returns to the people and places that marked me in ways I have carried around in my body most of my life. I believe our bodies are carriers of experiences. I mean to ask if there is a way to read my own past differently, using what I have learned from literature: how stories repeat and reverberate and release us from the tyranny of our mistakes, our traumas, and our confusions.

As Virginia Woolf noted in *Moments of Being*: "Behind the cotton wool [of life] is hidden a pattern; that we—I mean all human beings—are connected with this; that the whole of the world is a work of art; that we are parts of the work of art. *Hamlet* or a Beethoven quartet is the truth about this vast mass that we call the world. But there is no Shakespeare, there is no Beethoven; certainly and emphatically there is no God; we are the words, we are the music; we are the thing itself. And I see this when I have a shock."

I too experience life treading water punctuated by small shocks that change my life.

I am aging. I am turning around, looking back in an effort to gather and give over what I have found. At sixty and beyond I wonder differently than I did when I was younger. How I wonder has shifted, as well as what I wonder about.

What if we could read our own past, our memories, even our bodies, as if they too were books open to endless interpretation? Endlessly generating and re-forming and showing us new insights? What if the patterns and arrangements, the images and poetics in literature become part of us as we carry the burdens of our own lives? What if we could stand in different relation to our experiences? Could the stories we carry about our experiences . . . loosen? Fall away and become sediment? Rearrange themselves? Change form? Could I read my own past the way I read the books I love, with the same compassion, irritation, resistance, desire, playful transgression, erotics, joy, curiosity, and wonder that I bring to the books I love?

Could I read my own body and life that way, too?

What do we carry? How do we lay down what we carry too long?

While this is not a memoir, it is a space of narrative transmography. Like the body of a frog in a fairy tale.

Narrative is a shapeshifting space. Story space, if you will, carries with it the possibility of arrangement, de-arrangement, and rearrangement, as does language itself. If I step back into a story I have been carrying in my body about my experiences, it is possible to change the point of view, it is possible to curate the elements of the story differently, bring different themes or images forward or let them recede. I'm not talking about facts, I'm talking about what we do with events in our lives. We story them and try to learn to live with them. Anything that can be put to story can be storied differently. Ask any member of a family about a holiday dinner and you will get a different story.

One of the greatest transmographical spaces we experience in life happens at the level of memory. Memories are conjurings.

At the same time, memory is a mind-fuck.

It doesn't give a shit what you think about it.

Memory slingshots you back and sideways. It interrupts time whether you like it or not, usually through your body. A sound, a smell, an image, and your body becomes a quivering wobble.

Memory for me poses a kind of crisis in representation, where the desire to capture "what really happened" meets the desire to build a story that will help us get on with our lives, especially around difficult experiences, creating a kind of tension or schism. The space of memory is galactically fascinating to me. My interest was born when my father drowned. When I resuscitated my father after he drowned in the ocean, he lost his long-term memory. I spent a decade studying the neurobiology and biochemistry of memory in an effort to understand how the abuse he'd inflicted on his wife and daughters suddenly evaporated, how his rage and dominance transformed into sweetness and docility, how his acumen and professional skill as an architect underwent erasure. I emerged from that study with a fever dream that became a nontraditional memoir, as if the only way I could move forward in my life was to enter story space and weave a form.

I believe that memory inside the brain and memory as we experience it as a storytelling field carries within it tiny interstices or flash points where more than one meaning is available. In some ways I have come to think of memory as oceanic or like space. The way it stretches out or contracts. We enter into that fluid, vast space and locate moments that we use to create narratives that sustain us. We carry our memory pieces in our actual bodies. I often wonder what memory pieces we may be carrying from before we were born.

The present is both mesmerizing to me and simultaneously unknowable. The present just doses you most of the time, leaving your mouth open while you try not to drop down on all fours and crawl around on the ground. The present can take your breath away. Who knows what we feel in the present tense? As Virginia Woolf put it, "I can only note that the past is beautiful because one never realizes an emotion at the time. It expands later, and thus we don't have complete emotions about the present, only about the past." Eventually her emotions expanded so intensely that she filled her pockets with rocks and stepped into moving water, a detail that still guts me. When my daughter died, the only thing that made any sense inside the grief was collecting rocks. So in a way, rocks saved my life. I can thus easily understand turning to the magic of rocks to end one's life. Rocks carry sediments from all over the world, they change shape, they form or dissolve, they comfort us. The past realized and remembered can be heavy, or small enough to carry in your palm or pocket.

I've carried questions about memory as well as how we might

read our own pasts ever since my daughter lived to term and died in the belly of me. Her whole life one of a swimmer's.

My questions live in my body.

Toni Morrison described memory as "a form of willed creation," not the labor of finding out what really happened, which she called research, but a kind of creative conjuring. She also said that "all water has a perfect memory and is forever trying to get back to where it was," a line that lodged itself between my rib cage and my heart forever, and one that made me wonder: What about the water inside us? What about the waterworld of our beginnings? I've never been able to answer either of those questions, but I keep entering storytelling like stepping into moving water to *try*.*

Maggie Nelson speaks of memory as a strange palimpsest: "For the fact is that neuroscientists who study memory remain unclear on the question of whether each time we remember something we are accessing a stable 'memory fragment'—often called a 'trace' or an 'engram'—or whether each time we remember something we are literally creating a new 'trace' to house the thought. And since no one has yet been able to discern the material of these traces, nor to locate them in the brain, how one thinks of them remains mostly a matter of metaphor: they could be 'scribbles,' 'holograms,' or 'imprints'; they could live in 'spirals,' 'rooms,' or 'storage units.'"

---

* Then there is this reminder from Keats: "Touch has a memory." Heart crumple, huh? That one always leaves me staring at my own hands, remembering the hands of other people, too, living and gone.

   Marcel Proust famously mused, "Poets claim that we recapture for a moment the self that we were long ago when we enter some house or garden in which we used to live in our youth. But these are most hazardous pilgrimages, which end as often in disappointment as in success. It is in ourselves that we should rather seek to find those fixed places, contemporaneous with different years."

One of my favorite lyric expressions about memory comes from Joy Harjo: "Memory is a living being that moves in many-layered streams. It is not static. It is not a backwards look. It moves forward, sideways, and in a spiral."

≈

I ONCE WROTE a book about embodied memory, *The Chronology of Water*, and I agree, memory has no linear chronology or fixed note in time and space. The mind-fuck has to do with the idea that memory is both embodied and disembodied. The stories we collect and repeat exist in a kind of narrative sphere that is a little apart from our bodies. Ancestral stories, generational stories take on lives of their own. Memory inhabits us and we inhabit memory—as if there is a story realm we step into and out of endlessly, a kind of energy field that existed before we were born and that will exist after we die.

What I didn't realize at the time was that even after writing a book about memories in my life up until that point, even after researching and studying my father's memory loss when he drowned in the ocean in an attempt to understand what memory is and is not—I was quietly and masochistically still trying to carry all the bodies of my own heartbreak, my own stillborn gestures of love, rage, grief, and dazzling blunders. I was sticking to my story, unwilling to let the story become or move.

I mean, if I let them go, who would I be?

Take it from me. You can't carry dead weight for long before it drowns you.

There are bodies in me that I had to set down, stop carrying, if I wanted to be of further use in the world. I had to invent a process of how to lay those bodies down—including my own bodies of sorrow, guilt, pain—so that change might continue to get born in my life. So that I could turn toward ever beginning, so that I might continue to evolve my lifework in the world to be of some use to others. As Joy Harjo reflects in her book *Poet Warrior*, "At some point we have to understand that we do not need to carry a story that is unbearable. We can observe the story, which is mental; feel the story, which is physical; let the story go, which is emotional; then forgive the story, which is spiritual, after which we use the materials of it to build a house of knowledge."

These are some stories about shedding bodies. They are not a series of trustworthy memories perfectly lodged in amber, but something more alive in us all, something more fluid. I want to shine a light on places in the story where meaning turns. I want to bring you with me into storytelling spaces with these questions in mind: What pieces of our being are held by the environments and stories we have inhabited, and how do those stories inhabit us? Can being or identity move and change, spiral, like storytelling can?

These pages show you how I read my own embodied past, how I imagine a map for myself that loosens the grip that sorrow has on my soul without erasing my experiences, and how the map *moves*. I understand I cannot make a map for you—you have to retrieve the important particles from your own life that will help you story, destory, and restory your life, and create your own map. At the interstices of our lives, we trade stories and secrets, we take turns helping each other go on. May these shared moments and rituals for release and revivification raise your own sweet solaces.

I take with me four lines from four women writers as illumination guides:

> *Reading yourself as a fiction as well as a fact is the only way to keep the narrative open—the only way to stop the story from running away under its own momentum, often towards an ending no one wants.*
>
> ~ *Jeanette Winterson*

> *When I think of what I already lived through it seems to me I was shedding my bodies along the paths.*
>
> ~ *Clarice Lispector*

> *There is no such thing as repetition. Only insistence.*
>
> ~ *Gertrude Stein*

> *Arrange whatever pieces come your way.*
>
> ~ *Virginia Woolf*

A Before

≈

L: *So it's true? They wanted to name me Cassandra?*

B: *Mother did. She wanted to name you Cassandra.*

L: *That's a trip—I mean, since I turned out to be a storyteller . . . and hardly anyone listens!*

(LAUGHTER AND KNOWING BETWEEN SISTERS)

L: *Kathy Acker's nickname in high school was Cassandra. That's good company, I guess.*

B: *Daddy wanted to name you Eve.*

L: *You have got to be shitting me.*

B: *True story.*

L: *Well, how the hell did they land on "Lidia"?*

B: *It was Daddy's idea. Sorry.*

(LAUGHTER AND KNOWING BETWEEN SISTERS)

L: *You know when you chose Joan as your confirmation name, it had the side effect of changing my life, too. That's why I dedicated Book of Joan to you.*

B: I know. It's my book. I hope everyone understands that.

L: I think they understand that.

B: Do you like your name?

*L: Oh, I don't know if I like or dislike it. I guess it feels like me. . . .
It used to be, I didn't hear it often out in the world, so it
corresponded to my experience as an isolate. Then this last year,
BAM! Two Lydias in widespread release! Lydia Tár and Lidia Poët,
and a hurricane . . . so funny. But if I could have been a name that
carries a story? I wish someone had wanted to name me Undine.*

*B: Those are some huge myths. Eve. Cassandra. Joan. Undine. I notice
they show up in your novels quite a bit. . . .*

*L: Well, yeah . . . aren't we always entering some storyline that existed
before we were born, and will continue long after we die? In some
ways, storytelling is all I've got. . . . I can live with that.*

Skydiver:
Three

Devin Eugene Crowe passed away in Long Beach, California, on January 5, 2015.

My husband, Andy, love of my life, enters the kitchen and throws a manila envelope onto the table. We both know what is inside. In 2017 Andy did something either insane or miraculous. Maybe both. He hired a private investigator to hunt down the details and data of my previous husband Devin's death. In the kitchen, the details in the autopsy and police report sit still and safe on the table.

It will take me over three years before I can even touch it. Open it. Read about Devin's body. Sometimes I carry things in my body for too many years. When I finally do open the envelope, I realize why I did not want to open it. The opening will create an ending.

Twenty years.

That's how long I carried the body of a dead love.

I wonder, where did I hold his death in my body all that time?

Already I don't know how to write about it. I want to talk to him instead, to ask him questions, like those living and left behind want to.

I want to say, remember when I said our love would be the death of us?

Overdramatic, I know, but not half as overdramatic as we actually were at the time. Lovers in their late twenties shooting for the next decade like supernovas, echoing lines over time and the bodies of other lovers.

As I recall, he farted. I laughed. We drank.

I warned us, didn't I? No one listens.

I am thinking now all these years later not of Devin's death, but of the night I climbed a red and yellow construction crane. After I opened the envelope.

I did not climb all the way to the top of the crane, not all 265 feet. But up high enough to feel its shuddering through my whole body.

I climbed the core of a luffing-jib crane, and then I climbed a little farther on ladders up the boom toward the crane's ballast. I'd say it took me about eight minutes to lose all the feeling in my legs—which felt wrongly lighter than air—like a gust of wind could send me sailing. Vertigo.

I figured I had about ten to twenty minutes before a cop or some kind of security showed up to shoo me away, force me down. But no one came.

Night. Cold. Light wind. Rain. I wanted so badly to know what the last kinds of things Devin saw up there were. Like if I could just see what he saw, I could feel what he felt. He must have seen the night sky. Were there stars out? Or clouds? And the city lights, or at least the top of a city with its skyscrapers kissing the hull of the night hanging down like a cosmic sky-boat. But really, how the hell do I know what he saw? I do know he was shit-faced. The accident report and the death certificate both mention his blood alcohol level. And there was an empty bottle of Stoli on the ground next to his wallet.

That detail is hard for me. Vodka was not his drink. Devin drank Jameson whiskey and Guinness for eleven years, our years together. And cheap beer in between. Like his father. I was the vodka drinker. Like my mother. Did he switch, like he switched woman after woman before me, during me, and after me?

Up there, high up on the construction crane, I wanted to ask Devin: Was it beautiful, brutal, or meaningless?

I know the distance between those things: beautiful, brutal, meaningless. I have, over the years, learned to stay quiet when I don't feel anything or even less than anything when everyone else around me is claiming they feel something extraordinary. Look at that! Oh my god! I know how to stay silent and smile to cover my empty apathy. I've learned. Do not reveal your emptiness. I also know how to stay very quiet when I feel everything and no one else feels anything. Don't identify yourself as the one who feels the weird, excessive thing. Ever.

I look up at the night from my perch on the crane. I'm holding on for dear life, I can tell you. It is not fun. I do not like it. I do not feel like I am on a wild adventure or a hero's journey. My legs want to float, my arms ache at the weight of me, my hands tingle. My throat feels funny. But I'm no pussy and I drank vodka in the car for courage, so I hook one leg over the ladder rung to support myself and then I close my eyes and hold my arms out away from the ladder briefly. A bird pose with human arms.

Flash of full-body terror. But also: flash of full-body freedom from the burden of being with people ever again. Yes, it still lives in me. That feeling. Why not fall?

Was that our love?

I know how dumb that sounds.

We fall for people and pretend we don't know why.

Or we do and we pretend that we don't so we don't have to face ourselves.

I remember with my whole body how Devin used to say *one two three*, before doing anything difficult. Even silly things, like cracking an egg, but also very hard things.

I take a breath huge as night and hold it.

One. Two. Three.

Blow it back out. Close my eyes. Insta dizzy.

Did he feel the vast nothing up there? Or did he feel the vast everything? My love for Devin carried the same questions, I think.

Star or black hole?

Was it love? That was in me? Those eleven years? Or something else? Matter or emptiness?

What do we gain from tracking back to an old dead love? Everything? Nothing?

He must have scanned the tops of buildings next. Up there. Even if he was drunk. I look at the tops of buildings. I see a baseball on a roof. And some clutter or garbage or rebar construction crap. And son of a bitch. Look at that. A chair. Someone liked it up there. Even with all the weird crap strewn about. Sitting alone. Alone is a real place.

Was it cold, or hot? January in California I'd guess is fairly warm, but you never know, even California gets blasts of cold. Now I can look it up. I have the time, the date, I can track back because Andy secured the information.

The details and data of Devin's death.

He knew I'd need it eventually. It's one of several breathtaking gestures he's done for me in our life together. Most people will think it sounds hyperbolic, but he knew it was true that if I didn't know the details of Devin Eugene Crowe's death, if I could not read the story of his body, I couldn't live the rest of my life.

Is that love? That Andy did that? I think it might be. But love still confuses me. Love stories. Some of them descend, some of them ascend, some are suspended at least briefly as if they might fly, others plateau like a sentence that can't find punctuation or worth. Or explode.

Sometimes I think the choice to stay with Andy and see what happens next is the choice between life and death. The pisser is, love lives inside both.

Sometimes I think his love is the one that ascended as profoundly as Devin's fell. Stars crossing in the night sky.

Was there a smell? Vodka and deodorant and bird shit and city stink? Was he feeling angry and desiring or sad and nostalgic? The reports say they found DayQuil gel capsules in his pocket. Was he fighting off a cold, or his life? Was he feeling like a character he loved? That would determine it. Jim Morrison or Charles Bukowski or Jackson Pollock. Eyes swimming around in his sockets.

Devin was the character I loved at that time.

My arms shake holding on. Suddenly I am exactly who and what I am, a woman on the edge of sixty, three-quarters of the way up a goddamn construction crane. My hair matting to my head from rain. My boobs hurt—smooshed against the crane's metal frame and ladder rungs.

Here it is straight-no-chaser: I can't look at construction cranes anymore without my heart cleaving, my heart diving, my heart leaving my body. Portland has a construction crane about every ten feet now, it seems. I am up here clinging to this technological metal thing and freezing my ass off, scared as shit because.

I want to know how many seconds it took.

Devin's dive.

Or fall.

My knees swim. My arms ache. I feel like throwing up. Too high too cold too much our lives our love too much, Devin, but there is no Devin.

My legs shake like fractured sticks. I don't even know if I can climb back down. I start crying, heaving, everything about us rushes back in like fuck. We were in love, weren't we? We were making art, weren't we?

How do I lay his body down and remember the art of us?

How do any of us lay down the stories of our past selves and what we have carried for far too long?

DAUGHTER

Our mothers always remain the strangest,
craziest people we've ever met.

~ *Marguerite Duras*

*I*t's a common enough routine after twenty years. Andy drops
me off at the airport, I get on a plane and fly to a speaking en-
gagement or writing workshop to share my ideas and practices,
hoping to be of some use to someone.

Sometimes Andy comes with me, but we can't always afford
that. If I am flying solo, I always still tear up a little in the drop-off
zone, my heart still feels like a baseball even after all these years,
especially if our son, Miles, is with him; I watch them drive away
from inside the airport on my way to wherever—like it's the last
scene of a movie. The life of a woman writer, a wife, a mother, crisscrossing these states straining at their borders in an effort to help
people tell stories that might help us kill ourselves or each other
less often. Or that's what I tell myself, anyway. When I travel, I
always think back through motherhood as time and space, and
my actual mother now that she is dead. Since her death, airplanes

forever remind me of traveling from Oregon to Florida when she was dying of cancer, the last time I saw her, crossing aloft that vast terrain of west to east, baby Miles in my lap, how he puked all over me and I didn't move, even the flight attendant was impressed. I just looked up and said, this is life, with a smile, smelling of baby puke and sour milk. After that trip all travel for me carries life, death, puke, piss, shit, sweat, breast milk, and love suspended high above the clouds.

Flying, like falling, carries the trace of love and death.

≈

ORDINARILY, the Portland airport is deeply comforting to me. I'm sure partly it's simply the fact that it is my home airport. Maybe everyone feels this way about an airport. There are several other airports I love . . . and a list of airports that I secretly wish would disappear into the earth.

The Portland airport is just so fresh. If you've ever been there, you know what I mean. It's small. Tidy. There are wall gardens stretching and looping up the parking garage. The shops and bars and restaurants are swell. I've actually driven to the airport on purpose just to have lunch or a drink or hang out, as sad as that likely sounds. Often there is a piano player just beyond the TSA corral. Massage chairs. Micro spas. A theater playing Oregon films. Coffee and craft beer everywhere. So my sadness about flying solo usually subsides quickly, because I feel well held by this place, this liminal home that sends me off and brings me back. During the holidays I go early to get a good seat.

Usually.

This time, after I get through the security gauntlet, I have to poo.

This is uncharacteristic. I do not like to poo in airports or on planes, or really anywhere in public; I empty my body before I leave home. Pooing en route is just nope in my world. I have all these elaborate theories about what we hold in our bodies too long, what we expel, when and where our bodies override us. But my body doesn't give a shit. So like it or not, I make a stressful visit to the airport bathroom and poo and try to scour the anxiety off by zealously washing my hands. I never look in the restroom mirrors. Something about my own image disorients me. I don't even look in the mirror when I brush my teeth. In fact, I feel the most like myself when I close my eyes. I don't feel disgust or revulsion, just disocciation or something like it. So I just watch my hands washing themselves. I haven't been able to look very long at my own image in a mirror since I was five years old, about the time my father began abusing me.

Next to me a young woman—who looks as if she could be sixteen years old—wearing a giant yellow puffer coat walks up and washes her hands, then goes at it in front of the mirror. Applying makeup. The yellow of her puffy coat makes my chest tight. I can't help it. I have an immediate and visceral reaction to the color bright yellow. She uses colorful makeup I don't even understand—so many colors!—since all I ever wear is mascara. I only wear mascara because I'm self-conscious of my barely there blond nub eyelashes, no doubt a genetic gift from Lithuanian ancestors. No one ever taught me how to wear makeup, and besides, the entire concept is suspicious to me, but I understand I should not say that out loud. I sneak glances at her as she paints herself up, then rubs something magical into her hair to tousle it. I may be no good at wearing makeup, but watching someone apply it is hypnotizing. I full-blown stare at her as she takes some selfies, my hands hanging in the air drip-drying.

I am invisible to her. Increasingly, I am invisible to anyone. When you are sixty this is not a new phenomenon. I'm still thinking about how I feel about it. Sometimes I feel sad, sometimes I feel so free I'm giddy. I dry my hands off underneath the blower. I probably stand there too long because the warm air feels good on my hands. This is what passes for pleasure in the life of an aging introvert.

Turns out the sixteen-year-old yellow puffer coat is also waiting for the flight to Houston, Texas, because she sits down next to me in the wait-for-your-plane corral. We're lucky we got seats. Lots of folks are headed to Houston. People begin their cranky congregation standing near the gate. She stuffs earbuds in her ears and I open my book. We enjoy the wall of silence between us.

Somebody's mother. Somebody's daughter.

When the plane arrives, after they do the cleaning, after they get us all lined up in our chutes according to row numbers, she's still near me, near enough to see what transpires next.

Hot flashes are not subtle. Those of you who have never had one, you are in for a treat. You think you know what they are in your forties, and you think things like, "I got this, those other women must just be pussies," but by your midfifties you understand that those early-warning signs were child's play. These babies could drop a horse. Of course I have dressed in layers, because I'm a pro at this point. But my disrobing doesn't seem to be doing the trick. My stealth breathing exercises are worthless. Condensation of woman sweat blooms on my upper lip, between my legs, under each boob. I feel aflame.

The airline desk attendant says, "Houston passenger something something something."

Wait. Are my ears ringing? Am I dizzy?

The airline broadcast voice says, "Houston group one, something muffle muffle."

What is happening to my legs? Group one shuffles along, the beep of their tickets being swiped creating a nauseating rhythm, my sight blurring over.

The airline voice says, "Group two."

The three people ahead of me move up to the kiosk. The line behind me—I can feel the heat of them. I can't move.

The bright yellow puffy coat from the bathroom says, "Dude." Trying to nudge me forward.

Once my body decides something, there is no arguing with her, my body a human exclamation point, dramatic and unmovable. End point. My body saying nope. No way am I getting on that plane to Houston. My body is standing up for me in ways I can't.

I stagger. My knees fill with air and I can't feel my feet. A heaviness in my chest. My heart beating me up. My breathing jackknifing. Someone takes my arm, escorts me to a seat. Someone says something soothing about giving the woman having an anxiety attack some space. At some point the airport transport vehicle takes me away from the scene, beeping so that crowds will get out of the way. My eyesight is gray and blotchy around the edges of my vision. I do not get on the plane to Houston to do the writerly things. In some kind of airport holding room for postmenopausal women who nearly pass out, I text Andy to come back and get me.

On the drive back home I try to puzzle out what the hell just happened. Something about Houston, something about Texas, something about trauma, of which I am carrying a lot, or was it just a goddamn bright yellow puffy coat? Please don't let that be true. That's just pathetic.

Texas was not good to me. My mother was born in Port Arthur, Texas. I went to college in Lubbock, Texas. I was frat-boy gang-raped there. I entered the Oz of drugs and drinking in Texas. I flunked out of college in Lubbock. I was married the first time in Corpus Christi. I had two abortions in Austin. I was arrested in Austin, too. I was pregnant and on food stamps when I left my first husband, right there in Austin, Texas. Texas is a stain in me, like blood you can never lift.

But Houston?

"I just couldn't make myself get on the plane," I mumble.

Andy asks, "When was the last time you were in Houston?"

"I think it was when my mother . . ." But my sentence swallows itself.

Houston, Texas.

Mothers.

Daughters.

I'll tell you when. When I was around sixteen.

≈

MY MOTHER started drinking herself deathward when I was six-teen. She did not die from alcoholism exactly; she died from breast and lung cancer. But I am of the mind that that slower suicide called alcoholism was already a story growing in her body.

When I was sixteen, we moved from Washington State to Gaines-ville, Florida; my father got a raise and a new position at his archi-tecture and engineering firm, but the story they laid down upon my body was that we moved there for me, for my competitive swim-ming career, which was bullshit. So forgive me if I bypass that story. My parents are now dead so I have no allegiance to their version of that story. For me, the move was a transmography. I was moving from one state of being to another.

Sixteen was the age of mostly masturbating, of jamming my hips against a pillow every night, and living in Washington State, where everything is green and cool and alive and smells like dirt and mountains. The age of winning medals as a swimmer, dreaming of sex with boys, girls, dogs, anything. The age of no story but me and my body. The story of desire coming alive in the body of a girl before she is a woman who understands that the whole culture moves her toward her own lifelessness.

Unlike in the Pacific Northwest where I grew up as a kid, Florida brought the heat inside my body to the very surface of my skin until it matched the heat and wet of Florida. In Florida a desire began to crawl up my spine, even though I didn't have words for it yet. In Florida a girl teammate came home with me after swim practice. This girl was the first person who handed me a flask one day, on the steps in front of the aquatic center. The flask had vodka in it. To me, vodka seemed both the opposite of athlete as well as completely familiar since my mother drank vodka. I took a sip. My chest filled with fire. My hips ached. My mother picked us up. Once we were at my house, in my room, we took all our clothes off and got into my bed. We explored bodies. She seemed to be a more experienced traveler. She put her hands between my legs and opened me by pulling my lips apart. She sucked on my nipples so gently I thought I might scream, so I just whispered "harder." She had shoulder-length hair with the sheen of a swimmer. Her shoulders and biceps looked like the shoulders and biceps of boys our age. Swimmers seem androgynous until they don't. When I put my face between her legs I felt some kind of craven, ravenous hunger overtake me. I would say now that I was deep inside an ecstatic state when my mother opened the bedroom door.

The girl was ejected from my room, my life, my world, forever. I never forgave my mother.

I never forgot the taste of the girl on my lips, the supernova between my legs, the bruises on my hip bones that seemed sacred, the smell of her hair—chlorine and Herbal Essences shampoo. I didn't speak to my mother for two weeks. She didn't speak to me, either. Some kind of cavern opened between us bigger than that place where all of creation passes. But that was not the only girl between us, I can see now, if I take the story back a bit.

One night just before we moved from Washington to Florida, my mother got a phone call from Texas, her home state, where all of her family still resided. She couldn't hold on to the receiver—a real phone, those pieces of heavy plastic attached to curled umbilical cords. She dropped the phone on the floor, its dumb double black heads going end over end. My father picked up the receiver. His voice was more quiet than I'd ever heard it. He sounded like someone else's father.

When I went to bed that night, I felt hot. I felt like my bedroom was in an oven. When I masturbated, it was angry and wrong. My head hurt. I remember clenching my teeth. Then I bit my pillowcase hard enough to rip it a little. It was like someone else had entered the house that night. Or something.

The next day, my mother handed me a yellow dress she wanted me to wear wherever we were going. I had always hated the color yellow, and I do to this day. Bright yellow makes me very anxious and agitated, like a too-bright sun on a girl who used to faint in the sun and a woman who will someday get skin cancer.

My mother used to call me her sunshine magic girl; the color yellow was magical to her. It was a gift she was trying to give me. Magic.

My mother and father and I flew to Houston, Texas, for a funeral. My sister met us there. She flew from college in California. The funeral was for my cousin, Michelle. Michelle was dead at twenty-one. No one told me how it had happened, we just packed up and got on a plane. My mother couldn't speak and my father was acting all fatherly. So I knew something was terribly wrong.

I'm ashamed to admit that in that moment the death didn't signify much to me. I barely knew my cousin from Texas. My adolescence was blooming. I was secretly plotting my escape from the tyranny of family. I was a swimmer winning medals with admirable biceps and a delayed period. The drive of pure ego and the pound of coming of age. To me, there was no other story.

From the moment I stepped out of the plane in Houston, everything was heat and thick wet and heavy like a puffy middle-aged drunk woman who let herself go. Like my mother, back in her element, back to her origins.

My mother was born in Port Arthur, Texas, east of Houston, a land of bobbing oil rig heads dotting the flat-as-fuck landscape like so many Singer sewing machines. One of the details from her sorrowful life that actually interested me was that she went to school with the artist Robert Rauschenberg, only back then his name was Milton Ernest Rauschenberg. In my own life, later, in college, Rauschenberg and many other artists around him during his career were important—Rauschenberg's Combines with found and discarded objects, Willem de Kooning, Cy Twombly, Merce Cunningham, Jasper Johns, John Cage—male artists who influenced my imagination profoundly. The women artists of the age, Lee Krasner and Joan Mitchell especially, literally saved my life.

Of Rauschenberg my mother said two things: "People made fun of his big ears," and "No one knew he had an artist boy living inside him at the time." My mother was ridiculed for her physical disability as a girl; her right leg was six inches shorter than the other, and she had a limp for life. She often befriended or had compassion for misfitted people. Even now, it is strange to me that artists like Rauschenberg and Janis Joplin could originate in such a pinched and barren body of land. But artists can come from any body.

I was no artist. Not yet, anyway.

While we were in Houston, so I did not get out of shape as a competitive swimmer, I worked out in an outdoor pool when no one was there. My father stood against a chain-link fence and smoked while I trained. It was winter, so the pool was kind of "closed," but I was let in anyway. The pool temperature and the air temperature were the same, so swimming felt vaguely amniotic. I had to get out of the water twice. Once when a thunderstorm came up suddenly and my father thought I might get electrocuted, and once when he noticed there was a cottonmouth snake in the water.

My parents still hadn't told me how my cousin had died, but maybe that thunder and the cottonmouth in the water were signs.

What I remembered of my cousin at the time was that she had sternum-length silky brown hair completely unlike my fluffy chlorinated whitewashed blond nonhair. She was southern-belle thin and wore makeup and nail polish and Candie's high-heeled shoes and tight bell-bottom jeans and perfume. Her eyelashes were naturally dark and long and she wore lacy bras and her bedroom furniture was pink and cream colored like dessert. She had a Vidal Sassoon blow-dryer and curling iron. She was daddy's little girl—my uncle showered her with praise and presents every time he was anywhere near her. She was everything I was not. Including a woman. She mesmerized me like Barbies did—I could never manage to keep my Barbies beautiful. I always did something weird to them like cut their hair off or draw on their arms and legs with one of my father's fancy architectural felt-tipped pens.

At night I lifted weights in the basement with my other cousin, her brother. So as not to miss any training. Because I was an athlete. He was my age, and because we were both adolescents and thus rarely used things like "words" to communicate, we were sort of close. He had muscles. So did I. He ruffled the top of my too-blond hair sometimes. I charley-horsed him in the bicep other times. When he used the bathroom in the house I listened to see if he was masturbating. We were cousin close.

I didn't grow up around my cousins much—we saw them about once a year or so when I was younger, then not at all by the time I was a teen. My mother and her family always referred to my father as a Yankee. For them, anything north of Texas qualified. That was the story, anyhow. My Yankee father from Ohio had stolen my southern belle mother from Texas and taken her north forever. In our case that meant Washington State. My mother was the only person in her family ever to leave Texas. With my father the Yankee. Family stories have their own logic.

When they finally told me what happened to my cousin Michelle, first they lied. They told me she died in a car wreck. My face got hot and the skin of my belly burned and my throat constricted, but I didn't cry. It was an odd sadness. I didn't know her all that well, she was more of a kid memory, this older girl who was prettier and smelled good and swam like a water aerobics person rather than a competitive swimmer—long beautiful arm strokes with her head above water.

But one night my cousin and two other boy cousins—all born and bred Texans—told me what really happened. Down there in the basement with the free weights and a disassembled Camaro engine in the garage and a rack of rifles and hunting bows and wet Texas heat and boy smells. And Pabst Blue Ribbon.

Michelle had been dancing at a nightclub with girlfriends. At some point she left the club. Her car was later found all burned up in the woods—Michelle's burned body in the trunk.

When I heard that, I couldn't breathe. I went a little deaf. My arms both went numb. I opened my mouth, I think. My cousin handed me a Pabst Blue Ribbon. I tried to take a sip. It tasted like wheat and gasoline, but I swallowed it anyway. From wherever I was at in that moment, though, I could still hear them talking the talk of boys. I became what sixteen really is.

My boy cousins were discussing how they wanted to take the pickup truck with the oversized tires and the gun rack out with a baseball bat and drive around looking for who they had decided was responsible. I'd never heard the kinds of words they were using spoken aloud.

I'd also never heard boys talking about going out to "fuck some son'bitch up." Washington State, where I was from, had other lingo. At that moment, in fact, I'd also never felt like the ribs in my girl chest were clicking closed just from people speaking a foreign language. A feeling bloomed inside me that I didn't understand. I felt too hot. Way too hot. I didn't have the language then for the feeling; all I knew was that I could not sit in the room with them any longer without bursting into flames.

That's when I cried. I also peed my pants a little, sitting there listening to them. I started to feel dizzy and like I might be disappearing so I clenched and unclenched my butt cheeks. When my hand started shaking so bad I spilled my PBR and my crying became audible, my cousin looked over at me and ruffled the hair on the top of my head. It didn't help. None of my boy cousins knew what to do so one of them took me upstairs where the grown-ups were. I was crying pretty hysterically by then. Hiccupping.

My uncle who looked exactly like Joe Namath said, "What's wrong, baby girl?" My mother said, "Lida-belle?" The drawls thick and swervy. My aunt opened her mouth but nothing came out. My voice locked in my throat like a rock. For days. They decided the crying was about the funeral. Death. I tried to crawl onto my mother's lap like a baby might. She said, "Oh, Belle, I can't . . ." and grimaced, her disability—her shortened leg and crooked hip—making it too painful. And anyway, I was sixteen.

In bed at night I couldn't masturbate. I could only picture Michelle, her burned-up body, her blackened crackling skin, the look on her face as her hair flamed away, her makeup melted, on her lips, something between a scream and the word "mama." The tips of her chipped-off fingernails. I pictured her neck with black-and-blue strangle marks. Images from movies and television and endless streams of murdered women. A sea of common story spaces. Almost the structure of narrative itself: the woman in peril.

I couldn't sleep, I couldn't eat, I wet the bed every night.

Someone called a Houston doctor; my mother took me to see him. He looked like Boss Hogg and gave me tranquilizers.

Anytime I fell asleep I'd see something else. I'd see the face of a man who would do this thing to Michelle being smashed to a bloody gelatinous pulp, smashed by my cousins with a baseball bat. Left in the street like roadkill. PBRs littering the curbside. I could not feel where to put the violence.

When the funeral finally happened, it was hot and sweaty and horrible. All those southern drawls and black dresses and polyester pants . . . all that Baptist Bible talk and rage and sadness. I felt like I was in a foreign country. It rained that Texas heat rain that feels like a wool blanket over your breathing. I kept watching for cottonmouths.

When it was time to leave, the kids and cousins sort of fell to the back . . . and that's when I heard one of my older cousins say, "We'll get the son'bitch."

I wasn't from the south. I didn't have anything to do with the south.

But I opened my mouth anyway and let out this odd little animal noise—almost a bellow. Or a yawp.

I'm still wondering what that noise was and where it came from.

I waited to be punished, scorned, hit with a switch, things I had seen happen to children in Texas.

My father and mother sort of disappeared me toward them—unruly child from the Pacific Northwest who had no southern manners. They folded me up into their own story of themselves.

Then I fainted, which used to happen sometimes to me in extreme heat and sun.

Blond-haired blue-eyed child, oversensitive to heat and sound.

I don't know what my boy cousins did, if anything. But I've often wondered.

I never went back to Houston or spoke to any of them until after my mother died. Sometimes I think my attempt to go to college in Texas, my attempt to get married in Texas, my attempt to have a child in Texas, my attempt to build a life in Texas for a few years was me trying to love a mother I could never quite get close enough to.

I may have even tried to drink Texas. Liquid heat forever swirling in a big southern-mouthed glass.

I do know they never found the man who killed my cousin Michelle and burned her body. It's a "cold case," a phrase we are all now familiar with. Cold cases have become popular entertainment, in fact. The dance club she left from was filled with white people from Baptist Christian families Texas two-stepping their way through life. There's just a hole where the story of my cousin Michelle should be, like an open, soundless mouth.

Dead women filling our entertainment systems.

I've waited a long time to write about what happened to my cousin. Every time I crept close to writing about it, it felt wrong. There's the fact that the story isn't "mine," but writers are never stopped by that thin membrane. There's the fact that I didn't know her very well. My sister, who was closer to her age, knew her slightly better. I left my sister out of this story because I don't remember her being there; I don't know why. When she told me recently what she wore to the funeral, an image punched through my consciousness, one of her sitting in a chair alone with the dress she described—that's it. That's my whole memory. Sometimes I think I repress the image of my sister in my memory to keep her safe from the word "family." I don't think I have preserved Michelle's dignity by not writing about her unsolved murder. I think her dignity, like the stories of the women in my family, gets buried if we stay quiet.

What I remember of this beautiful young woman who was murdered comes in retinal flashes and sensory perceptions: Once my cousin Michelle meticulously showed me how to give a Barbie an updo and how to use colored-top pins for Barbie earrings. I just kept thinking about the pins inside Barbie's skull. When she left the room I cut off all my Barbie's hair and stabbed her whole face with pins. Though I did keep the doll hair. It smelled like Michelle. Our paths to womanhood were very different.

When I was about eleven I found her yellow bra on the bathroom floor when we stayed with my Texas cousins for a whole week, and I took the bra and put it under my pillow. I had no breasts. I had the flat chest of an athlete. All week long she was asking about that missing yellow bra. By Thursday, when her mother changed the sheets on the bed I was in, I was busted. But my aunt never said anything. She just paused midbite one night at dinner, looked straight at me, and I at her, and then continued eating. Mashed potatoes, fried chicken, green bean casserole. And iced tea. With lemon. My ears burned with shame. And yet I was not sorry. The yellow bra was almost sacred. I could still describe that bra to you. In detail.

No woman in my family ever showed me anything about how to be a woman. Maybe this is not a story about Michelle at all. Maybe it's a story about me and my mother, and her mother, and her mother.

I've never written about my mother's family, or specifically her little sister. My aunt's voice was high-pitched and nasally and the drawl was tempered by a kind of singsong quality. "You want a soda pop, *Belle*? *Lida-biddy-lida-belle?*" She was young and pretty and thin like my beautiful cousin Michelle. She was prettier than my mother.

As I've written many times, my mother was born with one leg six inches shorter than the other. In one storyline, this marks her as disabled. This time I want to tell you something different: She was beautiful—I don't just mean her face. My mother had an inside-out kind of attraction. She was called "cripple" a lot in my presence, but she was no cripple. No victim. Except that she was both. Her whole life. But she made up a self from the inside, and in its own way, it was spectacular. Like a work of art. Blown up with courage and color and seduction and delight and drawl in spite of an education tapping out in high school. Laughter and dancing in the face of violence.

My mother's family carries a history of small and large violences against women. But now we know that's a shared history. It's nobody's only story. It counts more people than it doesn't. And at this point, it's become a trope, whether we want to admit that or not. Pulling our actual bodies away from the trope is painful and exhausting as ever.

My mother burbled out one night a story over her vodka and iced tea about how her father had maybe molested his daughters—but not her. Once she said to me, "I think he thought if he touched a cripple in that way he'd be twice damned to hell . . ." Her voice trailing off into a drawl as deep as an oil well. She told me that's the way of the southern world. Or that's how family is understood when you are born into generational abuse and the customs that keep it alive.

I'm relatively sure my closest boy cousin ran into some trouble with addiction and the law. He and I have troubled pasts in common. His mother, my aunt, got breast cancer. So did my other aunt, her sister, my mother's older sister. My maternal grandmother, their mother, died of cancer, too. My mother died of lung and breast cancer, and when that happened, my aunt said to me, "Well, at least she's resting now. She was in pain every moment of her life, you know, Belle?" In her high-pitched singsong voice, a slight tremor to it.

"Yeah," I said, though my voice just had the flat tone and lilt of the Pacific Northwest. No music or wonder. But I knew what she meant when she said it. My mother had been in pain her whole life, and maybe carrying the weight of generations, too, grinding down one of her legs, crippling her dancing, eating her breasts and lungs alive.

My mother used to sing "You Are My Sunshine" to me as a child. Like so many mothers. It made me feel happy and sad at the same time—happy because it sounded like she loved me, sad because I was a kid who fainted in the sun, and something about that song never sat right with me.

Whose grief do we carry in our bodies?

I do not have breast cancer, at least not yet. I recently had breast reduction surgery, which I elected to pursue because my boobs were approaching Lithuanian babushka levels—a genetic feature of my paternal relatives. I just couldn't carry them any longer. Though my surgeon found a small lump in one of them while she was in there, the lump was benign. Before the surgery I kept thinking about how my breasts were carrying the north and the south—my paternal Baltic genetic code and my maternal Texan scar tissue.

Yes, I know that's ridiculous. It's the kind of thought writers have. Women, too.

I don't want to talk about Texas. I realize that I've written it pretty much out of my life. But I've often wondered where it went. Is it still in my skin, or voice, or breasts?

There's a song that's still popular in Texas—especially the Elvis Presley version, or the version that appeared in the James Dean film *Giant*—called "The Yellow Rose of Texas." Because I have, in general, jettisoned all things Texas from my life—my mother, my cousin, all my maternal relatives, my first husband and disastrous marriage, my college years, my first arrests, abortions, rapes—I never looked the lyrics up. At least not until recently.

Not long ago, an African American student in a literature class I taught was brutally raped and burned alive in the trunk of her car. In Oregon.

I have trouble knowing how to feel about what happened. I've always hated the way we teachers say "my" students. I try to avoid it, but I slip sometimes. This beautiful, intelligent African American woman died in a horrific way. She was never "mine." She happened to be taking my literature class when it happened. I'm not really part of the story. I'm abjectly sickened by it. I cried, alone, in my office. Wailed even. I went to her funeral and stood over alone by a tree chewing Vicodin. Trying not to breathe too loudly. I'm not in it. The story. Am I?

Her death triggered a grief in me that I can't find the name for. I was not close with the student, but we did exchange some kind of energy that felt like it mattered in that intimate student-teacher way, a little like mothers and daughters, except not. She was an extraordinary young woman. Her death haunts me.

I am haunted because of Michelle.

I am haunted because I am a woman, whatever that is, and the murdered woman is everywhere in art and life.

I am haunted because I left Texas as it is no part of me. I left my mother the same way—ran like fuck as soon as I could.

When my mother was dying she said to me that her only joy in life had been her children.

The last paper that the brilliant and beautiful student turned in to my literature class opened with an analysis of a Texas song. If you've never looked at the lyrics to "The Yellow Rose of Texas," you won't ever be forced to think much about them unless there's some reason to. The earliest known version carries a hard and ugly history. It first appeared in Edwin Pearce Christy's minstrel show in the 1850s.

The song's history is not easy to follow. The lyrics could be about a Black American soldier who was in love with a mixed-race woman who may or may not have been a woman named Emily West. Both professional and amateur historians come to different conclusions, in the past and in the present. The original transcription of the song resides at the archives at the University of Texas in Austin. It became a popular marching song for soldiers in its time, and continued to be popular as a folk song to Texans in particular.

Some historians say the characters in the song are fictional. The woman at its center, the "sweetheart," is other times connected to Emily West. Among my favorite books on the topic is Lora-Marie Bernard's *The Yellow Rose of Texas: The Song, the Legend and Emily D. West*. The reason this book captures my imagination is that Bernard unearths details about Emily West's actual life, which by all accounts was formidable. She concludes there may be no absolute proof that the song is about Emily, though some details of her life seem to be reflected in the song's story. Whatever her life story was, Emily lived during the time of the Mexican-American War. There are many versions of the song, and many versions of the story of the song. Folk songs, like folktales, shape-shift. Bernard's attention to the actual life of Emily D. West is much more interesting to me than the song, the story of a free Black woman who had a part to play during the Civil War. The song may have become a marching tune for soldiers, but the woman at the heart of it—real or imagined—resists erasure in my mind.*

My mother never sang the song to me as a child, but once I heard her sing along to the car radio when it came on. So she knew the words. She sang a sanitized version, a contemporary version of the song. The deeply racist lyrics from the time the song was written have since been replaced. Words like "darkey" have been replaced with "soldier." But the yellow rose remains.

The student's paper deconstructed the song by rubbing it against the grain of Harriet Wilson's 1859 novel *Our Nig*, widely known now as a counternarrative to the popular sentimental novels and mother-centered novels of the nineteenth century. Her paper was incredible. She taught me so very much.

Then she died in a way no one should ever die. To date, no one has yet been arrested for the crime. Lost. Gone. Like so many other women.

The echo is and isn't in me.

The deaths are not the same. But they make an intersection of deaths in my body anyway.

My mother's favorite flower was a yellow rose. For years on any birthday, or Mother's Day, or a celebration of any kind, my father, my sister, and I would dutifully give her yellow roses.

My mother was a quasi-liberal. She voted Democratic, she yelled at Nixon on the television, she was a March of Dimes volunteer

---

* Lora-Marie Bernard, *The Yellow Rose of Texas: The Song, the Legend and Emily D. West* (Charleston, SC: History Press, 2020).

when I was a baby even though she had to walk miles and miles with a painful limp, she campaigned for John and Bobby Kennedy. She was a working mother who partly supported my father through his architecture studies and career. When she said someone was "good people," she meant trustworthy. Yet she was riddled with flaws: Underneath her liberalism, she was threaded through with the racism and internalized misogyny she was raised in, like all of us, even if she tried to outrun it by marrying a Yankee. The Yankee turned out to be a man who physically and verbally abused her and her daughters. And her depressive episodes were all-consuming. Twice when I was growing up she tried to kill herself. She could have easily been a character in a Flannery O'Connor story or a Faulkner novel or a Tennessee Williams play.

At the same time she was also remarkable in her ability to seize joy—or if not joy, then the guts of life. I wish I could have seen her hit the dance floor when she was sixteen, seventeen, eighteen. From what I've been told, with her one good leg and the other, well, just as good from her point of view, nothing could stop her. There are no photos, alas.

Yellow roses originally grew wild in the Middle East, where they were used for medicine, ritual, and decoration. I think they drew global attention around the eighteenth century. Rebecca Solnit noted in her beautiful book *Orwell's Roses* that the mass-produced roses that make up the bouquets we are so familiar with today involve a complex set of labor and environmental exploitations. They have next to no scent, and their colors are often strangely bright and unnatural.

One of my favorite foods on the planet is a lemon. I like to eat them whole, peel, seeds, and all. I once had a dream in which I ate a lemon, and a lemon tree grew inside of me. I had lemon-yellow light shooting out of my eyes, ears, nose, vag, anus, fingertips. It was glorious.

≈

FOR THE FIRST TIME in my life, I truly miss my mother. For the first time in my life, I also understand she could only have come from Texas. Texas is almost like a schism, a scar running across the whole project of America, like the scar running up her malformed leg. As I write this, the current governor of Texas is attempting to take over the state's public school system, in addition to the continual sadistic control over the bodies of women, queer people, drag queens, and people of color.

But Texas also gave us Robert Rauschenberg, Janis Joplin, Georgia O'Keeffe, Selena, Buddy Holly, Cormac McCarthy, Stevie Ray Vaughan, Terrence Malick, Katherine Anne Porter, Scott Joplin, Richard Linklater, Wes Anderson, Willie Nelson, Barry White, Robert Rodriguez, Blind Lemon Jefferson, and Beyoncé. Though not all were born there, they each made a life that stitched through the state.

Are any of us "from" anywhere? I was born in San Francisco, but grew up in the Pacific Northwest, then moved all over the place. Does it matter, the state where we grew up? The lineages? The countries? Or do we all track back to dirt, water, and stardust?

For years I have been able to pretend that Texas is no part of me. And really, I thought that story was going to work since my mother died years ago and I haven't lived there for decades. I don't have any reasons left to go back. I don't even need to acknowledge Texas exists if I don't want to.

But if I return to the beginning of this story, the part of the story where I am getting on a plane, you know there's something afoot when you are a published author and you are invited to read in Texas for more than $5,000—still a big sum to me—and you get to the airport and find yourself unable to board the plane, positively crippled by the thought of stepping foot into the wet heat.

At the time, a close friend of mine said to me, "It's okay, you don't have to go. It's important to not go sometimes, so you still feel like you have a choice about your own life and energy." You know what I felt when she said that? Saved. In spite of being lapsed.

So I didn't go to Houston that time I told you about.

But I did go back.

Recently, my sister told me that my Texan grandmother—my mother's mother—divorced my grandfather after he went at her with a knife. He left and moved to Saudi Arabia to work on an oil drilling project. She raised her babies partly by selling vegetables out of the back of a pickup truck. Later in life, they remarried. Like a violence threaded through all the women in the family, stitching something into us we have to cut out ourselves.

I am in touch with the grandchildren of these women whose lives pulsed through that huge, complex, violent, estranged state. Women whose hearts were beating against all the complexities of the conservative South. My mother's sisters' and brother's children and their children found me from a TED Talk I did. They said they remember me as a strange satellite from the Pacific Northwest that landed in their world every now and then, and they remember me laughing and cracking wise. They sent a few pictures of me as a kid, and it seems true: I was laughing long enough at some point in the story to have a photograph taken.

≈

I STILL REMEMBER the paper the brilliant student who was murdered wrote with its glaring red A+ at the top. If I hadn't turned out to be such a lousy scholar, I'd have a superb insight to offer right here. Or maybe I'm just a skeptical scholar—suspicious of conclusions. About the student who was murdered. About my cousin Michelle who was murdered. About abusive fathers and mothers who both save their babies for a while and then don't. About race, class, and gender. About violence against women, about generational violence, what we carry too long, what we need to set down. About north and south. About mothers and daughters.

Instead, I've chosen to spend my life creating literature as resistance. It's where I want to put my energy, alongside legions of others who have given their lives to storytelling. It's the ocean I want to swim in. Which means I'm in the waters of grief and imagination, of laughter and rage, of bodies that do whatever they want in the face of all, of not apologizing for *writing through it all*.

Instead of a conclusion, I am trying to learn how to stop carrying dead weight, what to put down in the good dirt. I know about the ways death leaves a black hole. I know about how people come to think they have to carry that hole in them their whole life, generation after generation. What I have learned from storytelling is that stories move, the pieces arrange and rearrange, and that motion is everything, like the difference between stasis and change.

Instead of a conclusion, or proof of right or wrongness, I embrace storytelling again and again. I look for the places where stories and lives intersect, where the lines on the maps that divide us dissolve and shift.

≈

I DID GO BACK to Houston eventually. Recently. My husband Andy came with me. My wonderful editor and publisher put us up in a very swank hotel downtown; we ate a lavish dinner in the room on the big-ass bed; we went to an independent bookstore where I gave a reading; the people at the bookstore were phenomenal, beautiful, kind. A woman I know brought me a bouquet of a dozen yellow roses. When she handed them to me, my arms were shaking. We flew out of Houston the very next morning without incident.

But I will tell you a secret.

After the reading I buried the roses in the dirt behind the bookstore.

Houston, she rose like a sad country song up my legs, through my hips, up my spine, and into my heart. I felt heavy. My body drawn downward, toward dead things, toward decay. So I got on my knees in the dark behind the bookstore and put my hands on the dirt. I half expected to see a snake. The dirt said I should offer something. I offered yellow roses.

I said goodbye to the women in my mother's sad family and the too-heavy violence they had to carry, or thought they did. I said goodbye to the breasts eaten by cancer. I said goodbye to my cousin Michelle, I said goodbye to the student whose path I crossed mostly on her pages for a brief moment, and in so doing I touched the well of sadness that is all women who are brutally taken from this world. I said goodbye to my complicated, dancing, laughing, drinking, malformed Texas mother, her ashes scattered somewhere in the Pacific Northwest, now on a different, more epic journey, where north and south don't matter.

Sometimes I dream in yellow.

Sub

*T*he first photograph she ever took of me, she was so close to my cleft I thought she might penetrate me with the camera lens.

She said, I want to see inside this cave, this deep place where you say life and death have moved. She said, your body is like an epic poem inside. She said, whole philosophies and universes have lived and died where you say your daughter passed. She said, I want to make this cave a world. What color do you think it is?

I said deep dark red going to blue almost as dark as black. But I had no idea what color I was up inside myself. She said spread your legs as wide as you can.

She said now pull your lips apart.

I felt an opening that extended beyond what should have been my body. *Like the sea or space.*

Camera clicking.

I was twenty-six. She was fifty-seven. My daughter had just died. My mother was about to. I had fallen for Devin. Or begun my fall with him. Something about the word "fall," hard. I still don't know how to make a sentence of this. Devin and I were in our first year of graduate school studying literature and theater and art and performance and some days it felt like we might spontaneously combust with the thrill of it all. In Comparative Literature I watched Devin fall in love with Japanese Butoh theater. I saw his face change. I saw his pupils dilate. I knew something was happening to us. I thought art was happening to us. And our two bodies blowing open a world.

I also felt the terror of love descending.

When I look back, I wish it had been true that I would have done anything to sabotage that motion. Arrest it all. Unfall in love, stop his falling, stop his death, stop our love.

But that is not true. The fall excited me. The fall was everything.

The bodies and the art of women emerged from my studies as an alternative narrative. If erotic love for Devin was unto death, a phrase imprinted on us even in our wedding vows, then women were generative of life and art, a different storyline.

A woman came into my life who was a different storyline opening up to me like a book I'd yet to read.

She was a visiting artist at the University of Oregon and when I went to her presentation and looked at her photos I felt that I had fallen into an abyss, which for most people would be terrifying but for me was welcome. Like the sea or space, from within which all matter and energy emerge.

What was I doing? What was she doing? Was I looking for mothers? Daughters? Did I want her to be the man I couldn't find? Did I want to be a woman? A man? Did I want to be both? Man and woman? Something in between?

We nested inside her art studio. The bed rising only slightly off the floor, the elaborate lighting, the high ceilings, the white walls felt to me like we lived inside artmaking. Wine and bread and cheese and endless Billie Holiday Eartha Kitt John Coltrane Sarah Vaughan Nina Simone Charles Mingus Etta James Sister Rosetta Tharpe Miles Davis. The past opening up to me like a mouth. The music of the present tense fading into fad.

Her studio felt like a green world, an imaginal cocoon that I never wanted to leave.

When she first showed me the photographs she took of me I thought they looked like abstract landscapes. The photographs she printed were 24″ × 36″. I held them in front of me like windows. Rivulets and valleys and hills, canyons, caverns. Everything tinted the tiniest bit black and blue.

Later I studied them more closely. I thought they looked like electron microscope images I'd seen as a kid. The images were detailed close-ups, images of hair and taste buds and skin cells in *Time* magazine that I never forgot. I remember thinking *there are worlds within worlds within worlds*. As a kid.

After I sat with the images for an entire day, only then did they look like what they were, extreme close-up shots of my cunt, and beyond. I could almost smell them. Taste them. The black and blue tinges felt real to me.

Devin once asked me, aren't you afraid that someday she'll circulate some of these photographs? What if they got out?

What if my deepest insides spilled out into the world?

It was a question that had never occurred to me.

I was never afraid of anything about her.

Except that is a lie. I was afraid of everything about her. But it was the kind of fear that makes you unable to stop moving toward it.

She made rules.

She said don't talk to Devin about me ever again.

She said don't talk to anyone about me.

She said, if I see you in public, I will not acknowledge you, but you will know I am staring at you from the inside out.

I didn't care, because I was drawn to the rule of it. I was—at the time and ever after—a breaker of rules. The rules coming from her mouth were the first time and maybe only time in my life I felt a will to obey. Her commands did not feel like abuse, because we were two consensual adults agreeing to a kink pact with all of our intelligence. Her commands felt like a magic spell or a folktale kind of truth, or like we were creating a story and playing out the roles. She said, you can conjure any story you like. The way she said "conjure," when I look back, seems as if she knew that my entire life's practice would depend upon conjurings.

When I first saw the movie *High Art* I threw up. The intensity of art and desire making their knots is both the flame and the retching; the attraction and the abjection were overwhelming. In me.

Now she is dead, a sentence that lives in my body like an electrical current, electric eel, Tesla sitting inside his work.

I kept my promises.

In all the stories I have conjured I have never used her name.

Now I'm the one who is moving through her sixties.

And all the women I have loved both do and do not carry a trace of her. I say that because every body of every woman has some memory of her in the folds of flesh, in the expanse of a back, be-

tween thigh hills and the mind-loosening world of breasts and the
mythic journey of clefts, taking me back to my origins like explod-
ing cosmos.

In some ways I do not have a right to any of their names. I didn't
stay to the end of any story.

My mother's early erasure of my erotic experience with a girl
hides underneath every story.

I remember our first night together, this woman and I, which
spun itself alive on the Oregon coast. The night sky stitched stars
between light clouds and the moon illuminated the sea enough that
the waves occasionally wore white gems. We sat in the sand and the
night and the waves took the space where talking might have been
and she wrapped seaweed around my head so that my hair was a
tangle of sea stuff and blond organic matter.

She unbuttoned my red flannel shirt. Flannel shirts in Oregon
are as old as Oregon. I tried to inhabit a lesbian body, a lesbian
story. She pulled my shirt off and then pulled off my black T-shirt
that read *Frankenstein*. My favorite novel. She put her mouth to
each of my nipples so that they shot up like they were screaming for
the stars to take them back. She licked her way down the terrain of
my ribs and then my belly with its topography of scars to the waist
of my pants and unbuttoned my jeans. I was not sure my ribs could
contain the heave of my breathing. My jaw ached. I halfway wanted
someone to pull my legs apart so hard I snapped like a wishbone.
She tugged my jeans down to my knees. My ass ground down into
the sand. I spread my arms out like a femascular Jesus. She raised
up for a moment, dripping from the mouth with everything about
me, and then she placed an ocean rock inside me, a rock about the
size of a fist. She pushed two fingers into my asshole, and while she

pressed back down like prayer and ate me alive, every mouth of my body convulsed and shivered: anemone.

To this day I can smell the salt of that night.

When I rolled like a slippery and sandy seal on top of her, she said, No.

I asked, panting and wetted and delirious, Why.

Because I want to take photos of you like no one ever has.

My desire an electron inside her artmaking.

We went back up to the cabin we had rented.

I still have the rock.

Inside the cabin we undressed. I pulled things out of my pockets and put them on the bedside table, including the pearl-handled knife I used to keep the smile near my collarbone alive so that I could continue to feel my daughter. She pulled off my shirt. In the light, she looked at the unsutured cut at my collarbone and the knife on the bedside table and said, what's this, placing her fingertips there on my skin. I answered her. I'm creating another mouth for unspoken stories that live in me.

She said give me the knife.

She took the knife, sanitized it with her lighter, and said, hold still. I can hold more still than a dead person. She then proceeded to take the line at my collarbone further, so that it traveled down between my breasts, but lightly, so lightly. The blood droplets looked like the most delicate stitching from some brilliant seamstress. Then she took the line back up to my other collarbone. There, she said. Like the most fragile string between wings. Not at my back, but in a place where I could witness them.

My memory often turns the past into a present-tense flash when I think of her.

With her I resuscitate a self. She studies my behaviors for exactly three months. She notes that I keep rereading some books, like my copy of *Frankenstein*. She notes that I read everything Marguerite Duras has ever written, and that I am particularly obsessed with *Hiroshima Mon Amour*, *The Lover*, and *The Sea Wall*. She watches me write notes like tiny hieroglyphics inside *The Waves* and *To the Lighthouse*. She turns on a tungsten lamp to photograph so that I can see the art books of abstract expressionism more clearly. She observes me touching the pages; once she sees me lick a page. She does not ask me why and this makes me love her. Then she brings three books to me one night. *Drawings and Observations*, by Louise Bourgeois, a giant book containing the paintings of Joan Mitchell, and *Autobiography of Red* by Anne Carson.

To me it feels maternal, gifting me these books. If maternal could mean opening the portal to an endless creative ocean. I devour the books. I feel seen and heard and something there is not a word for. I feel born, of a sort. Or brought to life.

I read *Autobiography of Red*. The coming-of-age story of Geryon, a brilliant boy with a unique disability who is at first sexually abused in his family, and whose heart is broken by his older lover, Herakles, who becomes a photographer who both captures and then saves his own life.

The seeds of a future novel plant in my gut and heart. Though I don't know it yet. She introduces rope play into our nights, strange and perfect umbilicals.

I read *Drawings and Observations*. She takes me to modern art museums to see the sculptures, which informs my digestion of her drawings and observations. A new relationship between words and objects threads up my spine and intestines. The brevity of a woman artist's words, the fragmented lyric turning like a kaleidoscope, the primacy of her images in the small drawings with epic implications lodges in my shoulders as a way to tell the story of a life—with an invented chronology.

We cum in water together many times. The bath, the shower, rivers, the ocean off the coast of Oregon, once in the rain in a random alleyway in New York next to a passed-out bum. We buy the man a bag of food for our sins. Does he wake up?

I flip the pages of the book with the Joan Mitchell paintings so many times the pages look like someone has sucked on them, chewed them, slept with them.

After a year I ask her, can I story you? Can I, for example, name you the Photographer? Can I make up names? Can I, for example, multiply your meanings across time and space? Can you shapeshift in novels and small fictions and nonfictions on a page?

Yes, she says. All of that.

In my head I begin a short story that will not fully unfurl until I am fifty-seven, about a woman who meets different versions of herself on a train.

In my head fiction and nonfiction cease to have distinction, if they ever did.

≈

WHEN SHE LEFT ME the first of what would become many times to go back to her beloved New York I wore dresses and lipstick every single day for an entire year. The only year of my life I ever did that. My form of resistance. Grief. Rage. Something. I never wore lipstick before or after that year. I remember thinking my mouth looked like a gash, and I liked it.

When I visited her later in New York I wanted to be anyone but myself. I said call me Klara. Call me Brie. Call me Aurora, call me Laisve. Call me Joan, Mary, Emma. Call me Lily, my daughter's name. Call me Dorothy, my mother's name. Call me Belle. She did. It helped me let go of self. It helped me be a hundred different characters.

Do you remember? is sometimes a horrible place. It makes you think you can talk to dead people, it opens the door to being haunted. Do you remember that time I took a train across all kinds of landscapes and weather and people from the west coast to the east coast to come see you?

Do you remember the time I stayed at the Gramercy Park Hotel and I drank too much scotch the night before I was supposed to meet you at your favorite diner, so much so that I was violently ill the next morning and could barely make it to the toilet to barf and barf and barf, and barely make it to the black phone—remember when there were big heavy black phones that rang too loud too shrill phones heavy enough you could beat someone on the skull with the receiver if you had to—and I managed to get hold of a waitperson at the diner and I managed to describe you to the waitperson and he said uh-huh, uh-huh, yeah, I see her, and while I held my vomit in he went over to tell you that I could not make it and no one ever came back to the phone, not for many minutes, then just click and dead.

In my imagination you just took the information and said, well, that's life.

Now you are dead.

So you can't remember.

I took a train the next day to the airport and shit myself, which seemed like a correct kind of shame. A woman a lot younger than me gave me something like a sari. We threw my Levi's out the door of the train.

We did not live happily ever after in some love story or photography studio. We came into each other's lives off and on for a while. With extreme force. Like a series of supernovas. Just flashes in time.

I have written about her hundreds of times, each time with a different body, a free-floating meaning.

I kept my promise.

In the most recent version of the short story—it may be that she is the only person on the planet who would appreciate it, and now she is gone, so all I have is the act of writing it, strange hollow homage signifying inside an absence, which may also be desire—I gave her a name.

The story is not true.

The story is true.

She is in the story.

She is not.

I am in the story.

I am everyone in the story.

She is all women.

Neither of us are in the story.

There is only storytelling, which is its own existence.

In the story, a woman is aging, and there is an erotics to her aging, but I have noticed lately, not very many people want to read that story. When I think of women artists who aged I think of the intricate lines on the face and hands of Louise Bourgeois, or Georgia O'Keeffe, and how those lines for me track back into and through the astonishing art they created, like skin maps or skin stories, and to be quite honest I find those lines on their faces and hands so breathtakingly beautiful I want to lick them. The aging woman artist is some kind of zenith of being to me. The "beauty" codes I have inherited from American culture just didn't take on me. I have always located beauty elsewhere, not very often in people, or in people whose bodies are outside the conventional. I suspect this definition of beauty and the erotic has its origins in early images of the scar on my mother's leg, her limp, my adoration of her actual leg as a kid.

I named her Pauline. Pauline was my maternal grandmother's name, although from her birth certificate I have learned that Pauline was not her name. Some slippage of the truth occurred that I cannot yet track down. My grandmother's name was Alma. My grandmother was as tall as she was.

I wonder: Where is Alma's story?

What slippages happen to women in the stories we tell about them or ourselves? Perhaps this is the reason I am a writer. Over the years I read and reread *The Book of Promethea* by Hélène Cixous. Each time I cry uncontrollably trying to trace the love affair of two women and at the difficulty of finding a language and a story that do not destroy the love story of two women in the writing.

In my own writing, I have tried many times to tell this story in the first person. For thirty-two years, through marriages, through careers that came and went, through raising children into adults. But a certain kind of slippage always occurs. Something of my "I" always gives way from first person to third person or worse, second, as if there have always been three of us here in the story. And maybe that's true. The me who lives in the Pacific Northwest. The me who traveled four times a year to New York. And the me who lives between them, inside the interstice, the fictional me, taking her chances, a body generating thousands of potential meanings.

≈

A LINE FROM HÉLÈNE CIXOUS winds its way into the folds of my brain: "To come up with a language that heals as much as it separates."

We story our way through our lives. Might the stories loosen, lift, change?

In fiction, I can lap up desire and spit it out as saliva between lovers, some kind of poetic derangement, an erotic fever dream. Fiction allows me fluidity of language and storytelling, the possibility of losing sense, moving toward lyricism, poetry, even beyond comprehensibility to an unknown, ecstatic edge. In nonfiction, I can "just tell it"—though the limits of nonfiction make me laugh. How can I ever write the book of her? Like desire eating hunger.

SKYDIVER:

TWO

I only learned about Devin's death because someone—a friend from the past who knew us—mentioned seeing his obituary. She messaged me on Facebook. When I saw her name come up, I held my breath and whisper-counted, *one two three.*

When I read the idiotic obituary, what I felt first was rage at the phrase "passed away." I suspect this phrase was his mother's, or someone else blood-related but not intimately related. It's passive. It's southern, it's Christian—like Alabama, where Devin was from. It contains within it an image of a person floating away into thin air, dissipating, almost as if they were never there at all.

And yet we know that the phrase "passed away" stands in for a lot. Whole lives. The first thing we want to know, whether it is respectful to ask, is how did it happen? Especially when the deceased is fifty-two. That's not an ordinary death date. It makes us nervous. There's something in it that cut an adult's life short.

But I can tell you, deep in the fist of my heart, exactly where I'd hidden it, I already knew how it happened. Even though no one told me.

"Passed away" is dead language. That's how I know his mother probably wrote it. She also wrote about how he was a very strong competitive tennis player as a teen, and exactly nothing about the children he left in the world that I know about and carry in my heart, secrets with nothing but sky to look at where he should exist . . . children floating in air. Nothing at all about his paintings. The life's blood of his art.

You'd have hated that, I say out loud to no one but Facebook.

You'd have pissed on it, I say louder.

But I'm talking to thin air.

≈

I MET DEVIN EUGENE CROWE the first week of graduate school at the University of Oregon. He was the most beautiful person in the room—hands down. Seriously. The beautiful women in the room were a fade. My twerp younger girlfriend at the time was a fade. I remember exactly what he was wearing, even if I'm wrong. He wore a silk-back men's vintage suit vest over a black T-shirt. His hair hung down his back like perfect black telephone cords (I remember at the time thinking jesus, woman, surely you can think of a more beautiful image than telephone cords, but that's the image that came to me, crass and bold; I wasn't a writer yet and yet all of my writing from that moment on would stay crass and bold), all the way to his ass. There was a faux hippie rainbow thing braided into his hair. His nose was pierced with a stud. He smelled like patchouli, but he wore an anarchist ring as well as an Irish claddagh ring. He wore handwoven Guatemalan shorts and irreverent flip-flops.

He looked about as literature grad school as if the Dude had showed up, farted, and gotten into a fistfight with the dean. He looked like he was about to offer to buy the entire room a round: *"For all my friends!"*

But maybe his eyes were really the word for him. Little infinite voids. Like twin black holes.

I loved Devin unto death. If not instantly, then unflinchingly.

The dean was at the podium yammering on to us newly minted graduate students about policy, structure, something, but I had no idea what he was saying because I went deaf. The whole room was Devin Eugene Crowe. I would never say it was love at first sight. Like I told Devin, I don't believe in that shit.

I would say that I went with spectacular death that day.

I know it's unseemly, but just like there are some women who can drink like a man, or women whose desire is unstoppable, there are women who can carry a death drive, a lust for danger, as aggressively as any man.

That was me.

I was not afraid of Devin Eugene Crowe and he was not afraid of me. If we were afraid of anything in the world, it was that love might save our lives. And then who the hell would either of us be? I know what I'm talking about.

During the Covid years, with all that time on my hands, for the first time in decades I watched a video of our wedding. I have never seen two people look more terrified by a ritual so ordinary.

There is a way in which we couldn't have been more perfect for each other. Eros and Thanatos arriving for their close-ups.

At that time I was a walking dead woman using sex to self-immolate. I hated everyone. Everything. My whole face was a flame.

I'd just experienced the trauma of loss, a daughter who died the day she was born. I was swimming in the sea of psychosis and grief. Turns out, what I ended up using to begin my fight back to the surface from the depth of my grief was the same energy I used to get myself out of my father's house: rage. And what emerged was a walking anger and a death drive so big sometimes I thought my arms and legs might shoot off like missiles. Rage on a young woman can appear seductive. For a time.

Sometimes I wonder what we looked like to other people around us at the time. Did we blend in with the sea of know-nothing graduate students? Did we stand out? Could anyone see that my hair was on fire? Could anyone detect that he was a walking suicide case? As a teacher at a community college later in life, I certainly noticed the students on the edge—the ones not sure if they wanted to die trying to live or live trying to die.

We were standing next to each other staring at textbooks at the University of Oregon bookstore. I am positive we had the same cynical smart-ass comment in our heads: Go, Ducks. It is later that day. Without looking at him I said I'm Lidia. Without looking at me he said I saw you at the English Department thing. I said yes I saw you too. Do you want to go get a Guinness he said. Yes.

At a bar, actually, across the street from the college, we drank Guinness pints until my face felt smeared. He was only the second man I'd met in my midtwenties who could maybe drink more than I could. In your twenties, that counts for something.

Later, at his crappy college rental house, I didn't tell him I was already in love with him. I hated the whole premise of the love story as I understood it. In fact, I decided right then to never see him again. To never mention to him or anyone else in the world the magnitude of what I was feeling. I wanted him to fuck me to the floor, into the good ground, to bury me. I could see empty bottles of Guinness—like maybe thirty—on the desk next to his bed. That's all I saw. I didn't want us to look at each other face-to-face. Looking at all the bottles comforted me.

≈

THEY FUCKED. Hard. All night. All week. Bottles of Guinness like sentries against everything that was coming for them.

≈

IT HELPS TO WRITE about us in third person. That slight distance that didn't happen.

Because the next day turned into eleven years.

I don't perfectly remember the time between when my daughter died and the dissolution of my first marriage. I think I was married to Philip for four years in sum, and not all of it together. Our daughter, Lily, died two years in. I think about five years went by, five years in which I was underwater with depression from the death of my baby girl, five years during which my mental health wavered terribly, five years where I swam to the bottom of the grief ocean and many times considered not kicking back up to the surface, before I encountered Devin. Books brought me back to life. Reading stories of other women with their hair on fire ignited some kind of will in me. And writing—stories starting shooting out of my fingers with a fire I didn't even know I had in me. I don't remember what year my divorce from my first husband happened. As if the years from my daughter's death, in 1983, to the moment I met Devin have been overwritten.

But I remember those eleven years with Devin like someone cut the story into my flesh.

I never meant to become any kind of grief or death ambassador. I just wrote about my experience when my baby girl died, and then the deaths piled up over the years, and more and more people brought their death stories to me, so exploring the space of death has taken up a lot of my adult life and my writing. It's true that I don't flinch when someone brings their grief or death story to me. I know how to listen and stay present in the storytelling, or how to ride the waves of grief alongside others.

The moment death shot into me, which is to say the moment of my daughter Lily's death, narrative and time distorted. Beginnings and endings no longer sat in their assigned positions, nor in my body. A kind of circle emerged in my imagination, which is likely why I am so drawn to stories where time and experience and story-telling lose their linear moorings.

Inside the death space of Devin, I looked like other people from the outside. I had an unruly dog, I ate Pop-Tarts and drank vodka. I wrote papers and had sex with other students and professors, women and men, I drank and drank and drank. On the surface of things I looked like anyone living in a neighborhood next to the tracks, near the Owen Rose Garden next to the Willamette River in Eugene.

At night once a week I blazed up and I rode my bike all over the place, neighborhoods, parking lots, pieces of the college campus, the train station, but I would always end up at the rose garden, where I would pull out the knife I used to cut open the small line near my collarbone once a week and then use it to cut fresh roses. I let Devin into my bike ritual, into the black of night and into the wild abandon and into my grief, he entered it without hesitation, with the longest eyelashes I've ever seen on any human, man or woman. Us riding our bikes against the river and into the rose-bushes. With a knife and a flask. My mane of blond hair whipping behind me and his cascading behind him like a black ocean, my out-of-whack laugh into the dark our only accompaniment.

I wonder what we looked like to people sleeping against the river or in the park, or to the punk kids near the tracks.

What picture emerges from a point of view that isn't us?

I have written so many stories about him, about us. An American couple both resisting a love story, sometimes violently, and simultaneously falling for one, with equal violence.

It's only now that I can see it was the love stories laid out before us before we were even born that were violent. Impossible to survive.

I still have many photographs of Devin partly because he was beautiful, partly because we were inseparable for eleven years, but also because especially in those early years, we traveled. The photos carry my memories of places. That's why we keep them, isn't it?

Susan Sontag wrote in *On Photography*, "Photographs are a way of imprisoning reality. . . . One can't possess reality, one can possess images—one can't possess the present but one can possess the past."

If only the past would hold still.

She also wrote, "To take a photograph is to participate in another person's mortality, vulnerability, mutability. . . . All photographs testify to time's relentless melt."

That feels more accurate to me, about people, about the past, about time. I have never possessed an image of Devin. I have never possessed the past. Something always slips or hides.

We had no money. So when I say we traveled, I mean backpacking, taking crowded buses and trains and ferries, peeing and pooing wherever we could, sleeping wherever we could—cars with unlocked doors or alleys or toolsheds or beaches or fields or barns or lightless houses we broke into. We scrounged food at public events like art show receptions or random weddings, we shared a single side dish as dinner at a restaurant, we picked fruit or vegetables from country to country to pay for train tickets, we slept in the fields of kind people who said, yes, over there near the sheep shed. I never thought about how little money we had. Ever.

Ireland, Scotland, Greece—the Peloponnese, the Cyclades, the Ionian Islands—London, Paris, and the north coast of France.

It went like this: He'd say let's go to Greece. I'd say how the fuck are we going to do that? He looked around our house and said, we sell everything and pack up the backpacks. As if he was saying I'm going to go make some coffee. He could have said anything and I would have said yes. The more difficult the idea the better. I didn't want to know anything for the longest time. I didn't care about having deep thoughts, or personal reflection, or being mindful of actions. I just wanted to be in motion with this fiery force of nature.

He could have said let's jump off a construction crane. I was ready.

Greece was the epic journey that sewed us to each other, just like in myth. Hydra, Poros, Ios, Naxos, Kythira, Milos, Mykonos, Santorini, Sifnos. Sometimes instead of the word "Devin" I listed the names of these islands silently in my head. An Aegean archipelago carrying the trace of a chaotic or perhaps lost or maybe just right-about-everything-as-he-barreled-deathward American man who loved retsina and Metaxa and olives and oceans and staring for hours into time and space.

I believe that journey began our epic cleaving.

≈

ONE MORNING in Santorini on the whitewashed deck of our hostel as Devin was cracking a hard-boiled egg, *one two three*, overlooking the Aegean. I said, "That sound. That's the sound of where love goes."

I don't know why I said that, but I was right.

Lines from *To the Lighthouse* popped into my skull: "What is the meaning of life? That was all—a simple question; one that tended to close in on one with years, the great revelation had never come. The great revelation perhaps never did come. Instead, there were little daily miracles, illuminations, matches struck unexpectedly in the dark; here was one."

The sound of an eggshell cracking against a spoon. *One two three.*

Crete in the distance, myths of love and civilization around us in waves.

≈

THERE ARE maybe three photos of me from that time we traveled together in Greece. I have about one hundred photos of Devin. What does that mean? Was I just more into photography than he was? Did I love him more? Did I possess him, the way Susan Sontag suggested when she said "photographs are a way of imprisoning reality"? Did he not see me? Did he not care about capturing an image of me, and if not, does it matter? Was I just not the kind of woman you want to take photos of? Was he closer to something present and fierce and alive, and therefore photographs were meaningless to him? That would be a romantic interpretation of him, wouldn't it?

Who was I? A woman who is almost unseen?

There are a few photos of me. In one photograph I am barebreasted, stepping out of an ocean the color that defied language. The Aegean reopens your imagination to wonder. My lifelong weird water pull, or the ecstatic desire to go back to ocean rather than live out the rest of my life on land, electrified my gut and skin so intensely in Greece that sometimes I had a hard time breathing on land.

I can't believe I was worried if I was fat in that moment. That I was self-conscious about my American flab, my pendulous tits, my too-blond stand-out-everywhere-we-went hair, my transparent blue eyes, my I am not a young hottie with insufferable perky titties and a high-up ass like all the other dark-haired women Devin's eyes were drawn to. I looked like exactly what I was. A woman who should be dead from grief and rage but wasn't. A woman whose formidable intelligence and creativity were just getting born, only she had no fucking idea what to do with them. A woman in her twenties who had just been leveled by grief bigger than a body with a slightly sagging gut since I'd just carried both life and death, stepping out of an ocean from myth toward a man who thought death was a real place. One drink at a time. Leg, lip, soul over the edge.

I stepped on a sharp shell and cut my foot.

≈

I LOVE THIS PHOTO of myself so much I want to bite it, because I never saw her again. That me.

I also hate this photo passionately. It cuts me open.

When I look at this photo, I think I look like an undine stepping out of her better world, risking land and life, for Devin, or that's what she told herself.

The photo pings my vertebrae and hips and reminds me that I violently wanted a man at the edge of death. That I could not have helped wanting him. But neither could I carry him—the weight of him, the soggy mass and mess of him—in the end.

I tried so hard.

Dear Devin.

Dear shrapnel lodged in my heart.

Dear artist who fell or leapt.

Crow.

Crane.

Boy.

Father.

Sorrow.

Swallow.

I will never know.

I only know I want to wrench the story away from plot and action, into an otherwhere, forever.

≈

WHEN I LOOK at any construction crane, I see Devin. After his death, the cranes began to make Portland, Oregon, seem like a city filled with death to me. That's not the reason Andy and I moved to the woods, but it isn't nothing, either. I've had to repress what I feel with great force.

When I see a sandhill crane on the Oregon coast, when I hear its bugling, when I witness the length of its neck in flight, sometimes I think it's you, Devin.

In Butoh theater, the performers of crane study and imitate the crane's neck, its delicate slender. They imagine a wire in the body, the crane stretching out from its very internal organs; the neck must not stop. It is important to remember the crane's nerves being pulled out like pieces of thread.

Slender neck.

A neck making S shapes in the air.

Quick trances, quick contractions.

Staring at the sky.

Stillness. Plucking at insects in feathers. Left shoulder raised slightly.

A dance of fine lines, the lines merging cobwebs, the lines accumulating in the body.*

WHAT'S THE USE of returning to the story of a dead love?

Not to find "what happened," but why it matters. To find matter—that place where love and death kiss, that place of creation and destruction. To find the glimpses of art and heart in my own story, the small sediments that arrange and settle, then again rise and rearrange.

To retrieve the fact that I chose life over death.

Not to rehash, but to reshape.

Instead of whatever it is that happened, in place of an obituary, in place of any memory that might land, in place of him ending, I

---

* Source: butoh-kaden.com/en/worlds/bird-beast/tsuru.

imagine birds. Cranes, crows, winged creatures without names yet. Stories of flight.

The truth is, I always inhabited a different set of storylines. We went to see *The Piano* together once. I sobbed through the movie's ending, I sobbed all the way to the car, I sobbed for an hour inside my blue pickup truck, while he sat with me dumbfounded and irritated and drove us home. The dialogue got into my body. The image of the main character sinking to the bottom of the sea with her piano, then kicking for life back to the surface: *What a death! What a chance! What a surprise! My will has chosen life!*

Bellevue Public Schools

Student Lidia Yukman

Teacher Davenport

School Robinswood

SUMMARY OF FALL CONFERENCE,
NOVEMBER 13, 1969

L idia is an eager, enthusiastic class member. She displays interested, cooperative attitude in most activities. She begins work promptly and continues systematically until completed. Her work is usually very neat and well-illustrated; sometimes she draws pictures over her words. Lidia is making excellent progress in reading. She knows the short vowels, the consonants, and blends studied so far in all positions. Because of this, her phonetic spelling is also excellent. Lidia knows 10 basic sight words. Lidia understands number order and symbols through 10. She recognizes inequalities and the use of the symbol through 20. Lidia knows all addition combinations in vertical and horizontal positions through 5. She seems very interested in science and social studies. She is liked by other girls in the class. She has good coordination and performs well in P.E.; she is very strong for a girl. She needs help in developing relationships with boy classmates. She is easily upset during recess by normal boy responses.

Miles, my son: *Well, do you kind of hate men, then?*

Me: *Sometimes I do . . . or maybe I hate something in myself I can't figure out.*

Miles: *Because of your father?*

Me: *Yeah, I guess you could say I have a father wound that never quite sutured shut. Or because I'm mean to myself in his place . . . or I find people who will be a little mean to me . . . I don't know. That sounds kind of nutter, doesn't it.*

Miles: *No. It doesn't sound nutter. It sounds like you don't know what to do with your pain.*

ESCAPE ARTIST

*B*eing in Eugene is always complicated for me. I spent eleven years there, and in some ways those years were important years of my early intellectual life, my emotional development, even my life trajectory. Undergraduate degree, first marriage demise, dead baby girl, my studying under Ken Kesey, second marriage born into its own ending, otherwise known as Devin, first woman lover, first affair with professor, first affair with a student, PhD, first book of fiction, first scholarly book. Eugene.

Eugene is everything about the past. Thank oceans there is a present tense in motion, or I could not bear the weight of it.

We are taking our son, Miles, to college at the University of Oregon. We drove from Portland to Eugene. Andy is at the dog park with Sadie trying to run some of her energy off. My job is to go to Subway to secure some sandwiches for us. I'm absolutely pretending everything is fine even though my heart feels like it is dropping out of my vagina. This is the actual cleaving. Miles is leaving home.

Miles is inventing his own idea of home. Our triad is dissolving. Or that's what it feels like.

≈

I TAKE A WRONG TURN, of course. I remember the eleven years I lived in Eugene like bruises: faded under the skin, invisible scar tissue underneath. From muscle memory, I can more or less figure out where I am, so I hang a left to right myself, and suddenly I'm at a stoplight at Sixteenth and Willamette. My ears ring. The scar at the bridge of my nose itches and aches. My eyes well up like I'm going to cry, only I'm not crying. It's the past shooting down my forearms. My hands grip the steering wheel like something is at stake. The Vet's Club—now Mac's Nightclub and Restaurant—where so many writers went so many nights after graduate workshops, rises up in my peripheral vision like a madeleine.

How many of these little hair triggers exist in our bodies? How do we release them so that we can change, move, drive the damn car to Subway like a regular person?

In that moment I do not drive to Subway—I pull over, a fist to the bridge of my nose.

≈

LET ME BACK UP.

I once tried to get with a poet. Emphasis on once. I suppose I thought his intensity was about making art. Or I wish it had been. I wanted everything in my life right then to be about the intensity of making art. Especially desire.

This poet was wound pretty damn tight. The only time this guy's eyes didn't quiver was when he was higher than high and

writing poems, which, luckily, was often. Our epic breakup happened on a defunct hippie commune then called the Church of the
Creative outside Creswell, Oregon. Beautiful place—the land, I
mean. Gorgeous evergreens. Big wide fields. A natural spring.
This poet had lived there in one of the cabins for over a decade
when I showed up. His cabin was a two-story spiral octagon, built
by the one-armed guy from *Twin Peaks*. (Yes, I'm serious.)

I'm not entirely certain who I was or what I thought I was doing
out there. I certainly was not a hippie. I was maybe something like
a figure who was overdramatically, eccentrically, embarrassingly
Eugene, Oregon. Like Paris barfed up Haight-Ashbury. Sometimes
half of my head was shaved close and sometimes I wore a cowboy
hat with a FUCK GOOD CITIZENSHIP button on the front and
sometimes I wore a black biker's jacket and always a garter belt
and vintage dresses. I liked French black lace see-through panties
and single-malt scotch and Dunhills, and I didn't like mud on my
boots, and I hated tofu and vegetables, and I for goddamn sure
didn't like sharing a bathhouse with hippie folk and I never, ever,
went to the dreaded bonfires. The poet never successfully got me
to hike to the spring for jugs of water. I never cooked a single meal
on his campstove. I never loaded the woodstove. When I shat in the
outhouse, I dissociated while wondering about bears.

Who was I pretending to be? I wonder. Ideally, a spectacular
species who could maybe be in a Jim Jarmusch flick, but who likely
ended up more like Courtney Love. How many pretend mes have I
conjured? I wonder. And toward what endgame? I'm not sure I had
any idea why I was aggressively trying on identities, and I suspect
no one else does, either, except that in our twenties and thirties
(and possibly forever) we are trying to conjure fictions of a self and

a life that might help us carry our own experiences. I mightily identify with the writer Jeanette Winterson's assertion that we forge selves through fiction.

Who was the poet pretending to be? All that rage and fear simmering underneath his beautiful stanzas?

Every single time the poet dragged me to a Grateful Dead concert I bit the inside of my cheek while pretending in my head to murder one of those braless twig-thin spinning girls with their hands in the sky. Thank the universe for LSD and mushrooms or I might have hurt someone.

Once my blue Toyota pickup truck broke down while I was staying out there and it took a week for a mechanic to come. I felt about as trapped as a punk mink. I nearly lost my mind. I'M GOING TO MOTHERFUCKING DIE OUT HERE WITH A BUNCH OF TOFU-EATING HIPPIE FOLK WHO SHIT IN OUTHOUSES AND NO ONE WILL KNOW BUT WOODLAND CREATURES. The first thing I did when my truck was repaired was drive to Burger King to EAT MEAT as fast as possible. I remember making little whimpering noises the moment my mouth got cow.

But what I hated most about living in the woods with the poet was that the only available electricity came from a hippie-rigged RV battery and a couple of solar panels that could generate light and current for about two hours at a time. No television. No movies. Limited music. Almost Mars.

You probably think I'm being hard on the poet. On his hippie ingenuity. But this story isn't over yet.

What do we owe our past versions of selves? At what point can we tell the truth about how it really felt, without worrying about how it looks or sounds?

These are good questions.

So what was I doing out there?

I was out there because I was an idiot in her twenties testing my stamina at the edge of my rage and delusions.

I was out there because my father's abuse left a stain where my heart should be. If I was Eve, I was going to be an angry Eve, an unapologetic Eve, a bloody Eve.

I was out there because my baby daughter died inside my body.

I was out there because I was mentally and emotionally unstable.

I was out there because my father's fist—the blow that never came—I wanted it. Unfinished violence. Be done with it. It would have been easier to carry than what he delivered to my body.

Most of my relationships with men were at the nexus of desire and violence.

This is a place in the story where there should be a full stop.

I did not deserve the poet's blow—any blow, nor does anyone, ever. What I'm saying is that the space between my face and male rage was so familiar to me at that point in my life that I entered it again and again. Like a dare. My desire included a violence left incomplete, like a dangling sentence or plot. As if that was love. Move toward unresolvable trouble. That's how deeply someone who cannot locate a self worth loving drives down into self-destruction. At this point in the story I was my father's daughter, and I didn't care if I lived or died.

I told myself I was simply out there because I met the poet in Ken Kesey's graduate writing class, and I was drunk, and it seemed fun and freaky at the time.

One night Kesey had us all watch the 1932 movie *Freaks* together—to get our weirdness mojo going, I guess. And I was splayed out on a couch with a vintage crepe dress that I'd hand-ripped shorter along the bottom. The poet put his hand up my skirt during the movie, slid to the side my French black lace panties, and shoved his fingers up into the salt wet of me with everyone in the room sort of aware he was doing it but pretending not to be. Instant revulsion. Memories of my father traveling through my body without permission. Numb dissociation. What did I do? Well, you know what happens to young women who have been driving themselves toward a fist so they might feel something besides numb . . . I went into a hole. The hole of I don't give a shit what happens to me I hope I am annihilated so I don't have to think the things I think or feel the things I feel ever again.

One day the poet took me "sailing" on Dorena Lake in a rented sailboat he pretended to know how to man. Why do heterosexual men pretend to know how to man? Why do women follow their lead?

I remember feeling something like an uh-oh balling up inside me. As know-nothing as I was, I knew the signs that might surface on a male body moving toward violence: the little facial tics and shoulder twitches, the shades of mood darkening. The look of a man who is lying to himself about himself and trying to impress you with his story, a man trying too hard to be the tough guy, the charismatic doer, the hero. But I didn't say a word. I nestled myself in the sailboat and looked at him, maybe not adoringly, but like, you got this, thumbs-up, dude.

I suspect that's how my mother got sucked into the story of my father.

Zoom across the lake we went, all the way to the far shore, so fast it seemed thrilling. Let me tell you about thrill: When I was inside speed or danger or high or drunk, I felt alive. I smiled. I laughed. For a brief space of time . . . all that water. Motion. Dizzy blur of accelerating toward the edge.

But then the boat made a zany turn he couldn't control, the sail shuddered, and the boat tipped hard, sending me flying over the side into the waters of Dorena Lake.

I opened my eyes in the mud-thick water. I considered staying there, suspended in mire. To be honest, in my twenties, except for the charge I got from rage and danger, I hadn't yet figured out what there was to live for. Grief had nearly drowned me. I've given voice to grief, written stories about the death of my daughter, but now I see telling the story was only the beginning.

When I resurfaced, the bow of the boat he couldn't control was coming straight at my skull; I had to dive deep to keep from being killed. You will think I am exaggerating, but I am not. If that boat had connected with my head, I'd be dead. The boat had capsized, the white hull rising wrong side up on the surface of the water, its mast lodged in the lakebed muck.

When the rescue tow arrived, I refused to ride in it with the poet. Something between rage and disgust kept me from getting into the rescue towboat. Maybe I was mad at him. Maybe at myself.

What I did was swim. Alongside the towboat. An epic swim. The entire length of Dorena Lake. Miles. Arriving at the shore to a bunch of cheering boys yelling, *"Dude, did you see how far that lady swam?"* They high-fived each other as they practiced swearing. Took in the image of the larger-than-life woman stomping onto the shore, squeezing water from her hair. They didn't even look at the poet in the rescue boat, who sat hunched over and crumpled like a little man-monkey riding the rest of the way to shore.

I could tell the story of what the poet did to me next in my blue
Toyota pickup truck. Or I could tell the story of those cheering
boys on the shore, and how I must have looked like a wet Valkyrie
to them emerging from the water. They'd never seen anything like
it, like me. They kept saying that, shaking their heads, like they'd
really seen something.

What would it take for the story to undergo a release, an adapta-
tion, so that a woman emerging triumphantly from water might
carry the heart of the matter, instead of the fucked-up fist of things
that came? Why can't I be the Swimmer? Why can't a woman be
the epic novel of herself?

I'm already a little embarrassed to write the sentences that
way. I can already feel an editor chasing down my choices. *Don't
rehash.* I can hear my father scold me for bragging. *Who do you think
you are?*

I can't quite write that story of the epic woman swimmer, glorious shapeshifting archetype, as a self. But for goddamn sure I can
create parts of her. And so I do, later in life. She is a girl who
breathes underwater and moves around different epochs, or moves
epochs, in a novel. She is a revisionary Joan of Arc. She is a girl
from a war-torn Eastern European country who saves her own life
by becoming an artist. She is a childless woman missing a leg who
will move whole populations beyond the word "mother." I'm not
rehashing. I'm reshaping.

≈

THE RED LIGHT at Sixteenth and Willamette seems to last forever
while I'm lost in these possible prisms of my past—all the possible
stories. What happened was, the poet did not speak to me on the

car ride home, nor the rest of the afternoon or night, his ego simmering beneath his skin. I spent all night rigid, in a strange state of animal fight or flight.

I stayed out there in the woods with him.

Until I didn't.

On the night of our biggest, most famous forest argument I bet you could hear us for all forty acres. It did not sound hippie peaceful at all, I promise you. At the zenith I jumped in my blue Toyota pickup truck and ripped out of there. My intent was to drive to the Vet's Club in Eugene and throw my lip over a $4 steak and a shot of Dewar's.

But he followed me in his ratty-ass ancient red pickup truck with a homemade wooden camper. Because poets are wily.

When I sidled up to the bar and ordered my scotch, he did, too, quick-stepping it up oddly like something was pinching his balls. And when I glared at him hoping to set him on fire, he glared right back, making my jaw ache. At which point fate intervened.

A fiction writer friend walked up—a lanky Jewish guy I really liked—a great writer, a funny, self-effacing, brilliant man who, if I had not been trying so aggressively to self-destruct, would have been nice to me.

The poet decided I was getting it on with lanky Jewish guy, and he picked a verbal fight with him. It was so strange to see them go at each other as wordsmiths. But at one point I saw the telltale signs of steam building up in the poet—his dark little eyeballs got big and I saw his fists clenching at his sides. *Is he going to hit my fiction writer friend? Is this him manning the scene?*

All he did was yell "YOU." I have no idea what that was about. Just a word. Maybe he said other words. But that's the word I heard.

When I decided to leave I walked to the Vet's Club parking lot, I got into my pickup, and guess what. So did the poet. At the first stoplight he said my name, just the word, "Lidia," and when I turned to look at him he punched me a cold hard one right at the bridge of my nose. The blow of a male poet who was raised by an unforgiving, military father.

Snap goes the poet.

The swimmer sees stars.

I managed to say calmly, in the voice I am sure I learned from my father—cold steel—"Get out of my truck or I will kill you."

You'd think that was that, right?

≈

I WROTE THIS STORY for readers who are quietly nodding their heads yes. For legions of us who took the long road. To cross the intersections in your twenties. I want to track how hard it is to re-route the story. How hard it is to double back and find yourself—your roughed-up, rage-driven, mistake-making self.

≈

I MOVED temporarily to my friend's shitty-ass basement, hating life. I found a poem under my windshield wiper one day. A really fine poem. One that makes you catch your breath and feel your heart like a fist.

And an invitation to dinner and a movie—not just any dinner, not just any movie, but my favorites—filet mignon and *Blade Runner* and single malt scotch—back out at the electricity-challenged hippie commune.

≈

DO YOU THINK I knew enough at that point to not go back? Please. That wisdom took decades of unlearning.

I didn't know jack shit about men. About women. About not going back. When you are living the story of being bad, your origin story, the story your father laid down upon you—I mean, even your mother gave you black lace panties as presents growing up while she gave your sister pristine white panties—you don't stop to think about not being bad. You move toward trouble, teeth bared, snarl-smiling, *I dare you* in your head and heart.

≈

SOMEHOW HE'D BOOSTED the power, procured a television and a VCR, cooked steaks and bought scotch, and when I first get there, what's that in the background? Music. Not Grateful Dead hippie crap. Psychedelic Furs. *Crafty.*

Oh, and there's more.

The steak is quite good, actually, and the film is great and the scotch is superb, but I just can't get it out of my head that THIS ASSHOLE POET POPPED ME ONE IN THE FACE. What am I doing back out here? It was *almost* a moment of clarity. A near miss.

I'm sitting there with "I've gotta leave" in my gut, but when I stand up he stands up, too, and takes my hand and says, "I want to show you something," and walks me over to the bed.

I'm trying to decide if I can bear a "go numb fuck" just to close this scene out without incident. My belly full of cow.

He's sitting me down on the edge of the bed.

Candlelight.

Music.

Scotchpotheaded.

He kisses the top of my head. He smells like weed and Tom's organic soap. My eyes at crotch level.

He unbuttons his Levi's, and slowly pulls them down, and well, he's wearing—*jeeeeeeeeeeeeeeez*. I'm eye level with poet guy's junk all tucked up inside a pair of my teeniest French black lace panties. Giving me the strangest attempt at *sexy bedroom eyes* I've ever seen. Where the hell did he get his poet mitts on my panties?

My stomach suddenly feels as if it's filled with croquet balls and a thin line of electricity is coiling around my throat.

Look, if I was ever going to be with a man wearing my panties—which by the way is in no way a deal-breaker—at that time in my life it would be David Bowie, it would be Iggy Pop, it would be Prince, it would be some magnificent gender-bender icon, someone hot enough to pull it off—who's that dude in *A History of Violence?* Viggo something . . . or any number of gay men I fell for over my lifetime, possibly all of them. I lean a little masculine, so men who have not castrated the feminine in themselves are drool-worthy to me. But *not* poet guy, who just looked . . . oh god. You know? All poet-y. His pointy little goatee. His rattail hippie hairs. Like a man-witch about to cast a spell or turn you into a mink.

It was a nightmare except that it was also funny as shit—which is a really terrible place to be in an intimate moment. I closed my eyes and tried to find a little safe pool of water in my head.

The answer was yes.

Because a woman like me couldn't bring myself to humiliate a poet in his moment of repentance. Not with those panties. My panties. My choices laid bare before me. A man who just needed a second chance, or one who had just been misunderstood, or who made a mistake, baby I love you.

I remember hearing him say super-poetic things in my ears, but inside my head I was blowing up each line with hand grenades in my head so I wouldn't remember what they were. When it was over, I made myself cry some so I could get the fuck out of there under cover of feminine mystique, but once inside my truck I fucking floored it, leaving two wheel scars in the mud. I got a speeding ticket just before the Eugene exit.

That was the last I saw of the poet, as I never spoke to him or saw him again. In fact, I tried as hard as I could to banish him from my brain and skin and . . . underwear.

≈

HERE'S THE THING about the story. I don't really want to heal as the victim of male violence in a culture that is a dumpster fire when it comes to gender roles. I don't want to be yet another woman survivor—of my father's violence, or any other male violence—so that I can stand in a line with other survivors inscribed inside the same system that produced us all, reproducing us all, indelible on the hippocampus.

I want to explore the disruptions, eruptions, zany paths, re-wordings, and rewildings we might invent so that we can write ourselves out of this terrible story without end once and for all.

I want to prism my own past and choose a different story thread.

Why don't I want to quit while I'm not yet dead and simply give up on men?

Because I have a son who is beyond beautiful.

Because Andy is worth riding the story to its end.

≈

WHO MIGHT we become if we let our memories prism, if we let go of the stories that bind us?

The poet who hit me becomes my father who harmed me becomes every man who ever harmed me becomes a culture of men who keep the story of harm alive and dominating our consciousness until the day we make a narrative turn, enough so to realize that male violence is not our story and never was, there are endless horizons of stories emerging all around us, still.

≈

THE LIGHT FINALLY CHANGES, red to green. I seem to have loosened my grip on the steering wheel. I make it to Subway without incident, pick up the sandwiches, get back in my car. Out my window there is a crow in a tree. A really beat-up, feathers-all-fucked-up crow. *That crow must have had quite a night.*

And like that I am thinking of Devin, Devin Eugene Crowe, the man who came after the poet. *Devin*, whose etymology means poet. *Eugene*, where we met and lived. *Crowe*—my present moment. Language and poetry work like that—you can rearrange meanings, metaphors, multiply and disperse anything.

I can see the former Vet's Club bar in the rearview now. It was a good bar. Devin and I inhabited so many bars here in Eugene when we did performance art. John Henry's, where we did a naked number involving a bicycle and a great deal of bacon. I crack myself up because a colleague of mine who is a department chair in an MFA program just recently confessed to me that he was *there*. He remembers all the bacon! He remembers me riding a bike naked around Devin. Or Sam Bond's Garage, where we did another mostly naked number involving a trapeze swing and Shakespeare's *The Tempest*. My old friend Ty Connor worked there for a while, only now he's the bartender at the phenomenal Horsehead Bar. Beers at High Street with my beloved friend Bennet who has gone to starstuff. The Starlight Lounge, where the martinis are made with Crater Lake vodka. Luckey's Club with vintage pool tables. Perry's Nightclub, where I danced so hard with Greta and Paige, I fractured my tibia. All the good things that happened in bars. All the bad things that happened in bars. Bars: strange way stations in life some of us pass through.

Mac's Nightclub and Restaurant ("the Blues Scene of Eugene") has now replaced the Vet's Club.

If I could go back through my life with the poet, what would I have done differently? Maybe say something like, "I am not going to sleep with you now or ever again, and the night you hit me was beyond terrible, you should work on that in yourself, you have a deeply unresolved problem with rage and fear and your hatred of women—in me and in yourself, you have shadow work ahead of you, but this wearing women's panties thing? It's possible that's a good impulse, poet guy, maybe go explore that in yourself. Maybe you'll find something you lost along the way."

I remind myself that it is not my responsibility to take care of or even have compassion for the poet or any man. That's his work, their work. Instead, I think about my former self and her possibilities—I think about the epic water woman swimming the length of a lake on her own terms. Because she decided to.

≈

WHEN I'M CLOSE to Miles's new apartment, I see Andy and Sadie the dog making their way to the building. Rain falls from the sky. I park where I can—far—and make my way toward the building and soon the rain is a downpour, and I am drenched. No coat. Just a sad sack of Subway. I get inside and walk down the hall toward the two men I love most in the world, and another bar story comes to me, about the time Andy, upon encountering our friend who uses a wheelchair, sitting at the bottom of the stairs at a bar where all the writers had ascended to the cool second level to drink, simply picked him up and carried him upstairs. Wordlessly. And I have never been so happy in my life to drive to an ending—my son moving into his new apartment to begin his life and my soul mate who picks up other men and carries them. Even with stupid Subway sandwiches in my hands.

A voice rises in my head. I recognize her. She is my storyteller voice:

It's not your fault, what they did to you.

Men.

You are not the story of those men. You don't have to live inside their stories.

Men don't even know what it is to be a man yet, or how the story is changing.

None of us know much beyond the stories we've inherited.

There are other story paths emergent yet, for you, for all of us; enter storytelling.

When Miles opens the apartment door he laughs and hugs me and says, "Jesus, woman, did you swim here?"

Yeah, I kind of did.

MOLECULE

I once went hiking with a Valkyrie.

Let me say from the get-go, I'm no hiker. Not then, not now. I passionately love being in forests, in fact, I am now living again for the third time in my life in a forest, but I hike like a woman who wants to pick all the wildflowers along the way, speak often to animals and trees, sit down for a cheese sandwich or a forest nap repeatedly and without apology. In other words, I hike like a toddler. But on more than one occasion, a Valkyrie has shown up in my life and asked me to go on a hike, and I have said yes before my brain can stop me. I also passionately love strong brilliant women. Forever. Blame my older sister. Blame the fact that in addition to being strong and brilliant, my older sister first introduced me to Joan of Arc, Mary Shelley, Virginia Woolf, Antigone.

Once we took the Valkyrie's favorite loop through the Sawtooth Mountains. The fact that she had a favorite loop should tell you something about her level of hiking expertise. I had to ask her recently what route we took all those years ago so that I might relate this story. Apparently, we began at Redfish Lake. We hiked to the Cramer Lakes, over Cramer Pass to Virginia and Edna Lakes, over another pass, then down to Toxaway and Alice Lakes, finally walking out days later at Pettit Lake. Those may look like normal sentences, but that's a lot of hiking for a water creature, over actual mountain passes, into wilderness both steep and high. We saw no other humans for several days.

I should have told this part of the story first: I was in love with the Valkyrie. But the love was like a giant space of confusion. What did I know about love? We've been lied to mightily when it comes to love stories. The plots are impossible to live up to. Someday maybe we'll figure out what the hell love is. The Valkyrie loved me, too, deeply, she still does after all these years I'd wager, but at the time, the Valkyrie said a sentence to me that threw me. She said, "And even if I was a lesbian, you are, sadly, not my type." She said this to me with complete certainty, the way only an older woman speaking to a younger woman can. There was another woman around at the time who was her type, a woman who left flowers on the Valkyrie's bike one day, and I ground my teeth at night with jealousy.

I was not a lesbian, either. Or I was a failed lesbian. To this day I don't know what I am, although the "queer" umbrella has expanded enough that I might at least stand near it and shuffle my feet. I've rarely encountered the exact word or true space for my own stubborn sexuality, and that may be why I'm not easily embraced by any community. I've slept with heterosexual men and women, with gender-fluid folk, with trans people, asexual people, gay men (one of the top three most erotic experiences of my life happened with two gay men who made me forget not only the word "woman" but the entire English language), lesbian women, pansexual humans. Who you have sex with is just who you have sex with. The gender you embrace, the sexual orientation you identify with, those are yours, and none of us entirely agree on what words to use. I've loved many different humans. I don't fall in love with genders. Love goes wherever it wants to. I am of the opinion that language must ever-expand so that more stories might emerge.

I find all bodies eternally fascinating. Every size and shape. Every ability. Every gender. The word that comes closest is probably "water."

I do experience deep eroticism and ecstatic states from books, art, trees, and water.

When I am near seals in the ocean, I feel called, kindred. I've no idea what that is about. I am fond of the word "aquanaut."

Mostly I think gender is a false fiction we've been given, and sexuality is the ocean.

When I fall, I mostly fall for imaginations or creativity. The sound of a cello. A paint stroke. A story or poem that gives you an ecstatic experience. A dance. A single sentence. Someone who makes me face sorrow and still swoon. Someone who tickles me into laughter.

I fell for the Valkyrie's eyes—or more precisely, the tiny lines around her eyes that held the light blue of her eyes like perfectly woven nests. The obstacle the Valkyrie presented confused me. For several years. I could not have loved her more, but there wasn't anywhere to put it exactly, because of the sentence she said to me, like facing a closed door. For a while in my youth, I mistakenly thought who you fucked was your gender, your sexuality, your love.

To my credit, then as now, whether or not I actually have sex with someone doesn't negate or inhibit my erotic experiences with them. Spock and I could have gotten hot and heavy with that hand-to-the-temple mind meld thing. I believe sexuality is omnipresent and takes a million forms, some tiny as molecules, others epic as myths. So this story is either about a "hike" or about sexuality.

"We are going to hike the Sawtooths," the Valkyrie said to me. In my body, that sentence transformed into "Be with the Valkyrie alone for many days and nights in the mountains near astonishingly clear lakes surrounded by animals that could eat you." I was all in. Because Valkyrie.

Every time I have fallen for someone, I have experienced bodily wounding. The first woman I fell for, I broke my ankle. When I fell for my first husband, I fainted. The second woman I fell in love with resulted in a traumatic head wound for her and a knife cut for me in the place where I now have back flab. When I fell for my second husband, during our first month together I fell off a train—into gravel. When I fell for my third husband, I had a head-on collision in my car. With the Valkyrie, I bloodied my feet so much they looked like tenderized meat.

The Sawtooth mountain range is in the Rocky Mountains of central Idaho near Ketchum. Around 670 square miles, the Sawtooths are so named for the fifty-seven peaks jutting up, all between 10,000 and 10,751 feet in elevation. Over three hundred high mountain lakes dapple their wilderness.

Keep in mind cheese-sandwich-and-nap-loving Lidia.

Keep in mind the image of my abusive and domineering father taking his family of three little women—a mother with a severe disability that affected her ability to walk and the two daughters he abused—on "hikes" we could not handle during many camping trips from hell.

Within two hours of the hike in the Sawtooths, my feet were covered in blisters. My borrowed boots did not fit. And I have mermaid feet: soft and too tender and meant for water, I suspect. Our backpacks weighed around thirty pounds each. I'd never carried a backpack with any kind of weight in it in my life. The trail grades were 10 percent almost immediately, and only increased by the hour. I am a flatlander. Altitude is not my friend. If I spend more than two days in Denver I get a nosebleed and nausea and faint occasionally. By the end of the first day of hiking, my feet were unrecognizable. When we made our camp next to idyllic Alpine Lake, I took my boots off and my socks off and my feet were bloody as hell. I stuck them in the lake water so the Valkyrie would not see them. The lake water was ice cold. When I pulled my feet back out, they were blue, numb, *and* bleeding.

"Oh my god," the Valkyrie said. "Are you okay?" I mumbled something about bears while she tied her bloodied tampon in a bag up on a tree limb. The Valkyrie had actual knowledge and experience. I just had bloody feet and bear fear.

The tampons-in-a-bag trick was one of ten thousand skills I learned from observing the wonder of the Valkyrie. Most mesmerizing to me was her ability to read topographical maps with lyric grace, like she was playing a violin; I watched her fingers trace the lines, paths, and elevations; every once in a while she'd look up and scan the terrain and process exactly where we were, precisely where we were going, or she'd look up to study arcs made by eagles and hawks. I could tell from watching her zigzag on the trails' switchbacks that her body carried memories of this place. Her parents owned a place in Ketchum so she'd likely hiked this loop a hundred times—in fact, her mother did the first few miles with us, which secretly made me cry. What might my life have been if I'd had a mother who could hike the Sawtooths? I hiked behind the Valkyrie so I studied everything about her body. Her feet and legs so sure. Mine all wobble and teeter, stumble and fuck. She had a keen eye for all weather, when it was coming, when to take shelter, when to run or make a break for a treeline. Her compass reading was impeccable.

The Valkyrie packed our backpacks, too—sunscreen and insulation clothing. Flashlights and headlamps and spare batteries. First aid supplies. Butane lighters and waterproof matches. More than one knife. Small mobile repair tools. Nuts and chocolate and jerky and ready-to-eat meal packs. Coffee for campfire coffee. Water. Tarps. Moleskin for blisters, which we ran through in two days. Two whistles. Sleeping bags. Tent. The Valkyrie also knew all manner of details about plants—some could be used for medicine, some you could eat, others could kill you.

My ideas about the wilderness came from books and television and film and camping trips with my stupid abusive father and my disabled mother who, to her credit, tried to hike anyway on our camping trips, a fact that I now hold in very high esteem. Those hikes must have been excruciating for her. I never heard her complain even once. But the image of the Valkyrie's mother—her hair white, her skin speckled and marked, her face weathered as a mountain range—lodged inside my skull. A mother who would travel with you and ensure a safe journey up ahead, who would be there upon your return with a hot bath and a martini and a well-made bed, instead of a mother who drowned herself in giant tumblers of vodka, leaving her daughter vulnerable.

My Valkyrie was older than me, almost as old as my sister. What might my life have been if a Valkyrie sister had taken me with her when she left home forever? I'm embarrassed to say this was another thought that planted itself in me before I could stop it. These woman-to-woman relationships I never had but longed for. Mysterious and completely foreign to me, although I loved my sister more than anyone in the world, even in her leaving home, even in her absence.

I may have loved absence-as-woman. Narratives can get all tangled in our heads by our hearts.

The first day of the hike we covered about seven miles, more than I had ever hiked in my life.

The second day of the hike I swallowed a great deal of Tylenol, I cried without making a single sound, and my feet began to feel like hacked-up wooden stubs.

The third day of the hike the Valkyrie put my hiking boots in her backpack and literally forged new "shoes" for me from a pair of her flip-flops and some twine. I looked like Fred Flintstone.

We hiked thirteen miles the third day.

Every so often the Valkyrie would turn back and look for me. I slipped farther and farther behind, but I could see her ahead of me, squinting, hand on one hip, watching, until I was close enough that she felt comfortable continuing. My legs were not hiker's legs. My legs were not weak, they were just meant for water. I had breaststroker's legs. Like a frog.

I felt like a terrible burden, the younger sister who cried too much and was afraid of everything. I felt feeble. Weak. Crippled. I wondered if that was what my mother felt about herself her whole life.

But I also felt something else out in the grand wilderness so much more vast than me. I felt kindred. Kindred with dirt. With

trees. With rocks and seeds and water. One night while the Valkyrie went off to find some kindling, I put a tiny handful of dirt in my
mouth and swallowed.

Dirt:

*A girl of ten sits in the dirt underneath a tree in a vacant lot. Her
sister was gone from the house forever, gone to young adulthood, to
college, to a life in the world much bigger than the house. The vacant
lot holds the girl well. She can hear birds always. She can hear wind
in tree branches. She has climbed a western hemlock she has climbed
a Douglas fir she has climbed an ash tree while she waited for her
mother to come home from selling real estate, which she'd been doing
successfully ever since she can remember. There is one huge tree she
gravitates toward for safety. She sits underneath it. She places both
hands down on the dirt, closes her eyes, and says I love you dirt. Then
she claws up her right hand and cups some dirt, opens her eyes, stares
at the dirt, and with a kind of small calm and tenderness, feeds herself. Dirt. The dirt tastes like the trees, leaves, and like the roots of the
trees smell. Eating the dirt makes numbers in her head. A nine. An
eleven. Thirty-three. The girl is terrible at math in school, but images of numbers are secretly beautiful to her, like a magical language
only she can see.*

Seeds:

Do not eat the seeds inside apples. Do not eat the core.
*Do not eat the seeds inside of a lemon. No one just bites into a
lemon. Stop that.*

Do not eat cherry pits, the seeds in pine cones, do not eat winged seeds, helicopter seeds, those beautiful flying whirlybirds known as samaras, no matter how breathtaking they are to you, no matter how magical, no matter your secret suspicion they could change everything around you.

She eats them all when no one is looking. She hopes a tree grows inside of her. She hopes branches shoot out of her arms and legs. She hopes she becomes taller than a father or a family or a house. She hopes cherry blossom. She hopes lemon light.

Rocks:

She can't not touch them. She can't not want them all around her. She can't stop putting rocks in her pockets rocks in her shoes rocks in her mouth. She can't not want to be the rocks. She can't stand the rocks as an outside and some kind of inside where rocks are not. The rocks comfort her more than a mother more than a sister more than whatever a friend is more than God, who never comforted her, not once, who just seemed like another old rageful man who lives in the sky. Inside her there is a calling, like a voice among more than one voice. Different from the other voices, one voice whispers, almost like wind blowing through leaves. The whisper voice lives in her belly and wants company, specifically the company of rocks, a bellyful of rocks, but she knows not to do that or she will be punished, so she eats only the smallest, smoothest rocks, and only one at a time, and she waits many days and nights between rocks, sometimes a year. One time a rock comes out in her poop. She does not know if she should be sad that the rock left its home in her belly, or if she should be happy that the rock made a journey through her and is now leaving home;

either way she cries and begins to look for a new rock. Sometimes she thinks of the nine rocks—the total amount of rocks she remembers eating—she knows the shape and size and color and taste of each, how different they were from each other, how some left her body and others perhaps did not, how her inner ear has a small cup called a utricle that has a thousand little rocks made of calcium carbonate, the tiny rocks stimulating nerve cells, sending signals to the brain, what is up, what is down.

Pennies:

Copper and blood. When you bite the inside of your own cheek when he is yelling you begin to think about pennies before you can stop yourself. He is raging you are disappearing. You run and hide hoping to not disappear forever, you run to your bedroom and hide underneath the bed where you have hidden the pennies, the pennies you are not allowed to eat because god damn it that could choke you don't you know that could kill you that could make you vomit that penny could make you drool or gag or suffocate do you want to die do you want to have a surgery where they cut it out of you? But you know a secret that he does not: the pennies are smarter than he is. The pennies have figured out how to go from something of value to a nothingness that's worth a lot—their beautiful copper color carrying old dates from history and Lincoln and Liberty and an Indian head and a Flying Eagle and Wheat. Under the bed you put one in your mouth as he rages at your mother or at the walls or at his own small worthlessness. Under the bed in your mouth it might taste like blood it might taste like copper it tastes real. He collects pennies in a giant glass jar in the kitchen sometimes he and your mother pour them out

onto a table and look for old cents. You close your eyes and swallow.
You make a wish.

Paper:

Cut the pieces and make a snowflake. Draw a tree and talk to the
image. Draw a face without a mouth. Write words or maybe they are
not words write them anyway. Crumple paper trying to make rock
paper scissors come to life, try to make paper your friend inside the
alone. In a bathroom in a hospital in Seattle, Washington, when you
are thirteen and your teammate who like you swims breaststroke is
dying of leukemia after you visit his bedside and become deaf and
dumb staring at long strands of barely there white hair from chemo-
therapy eat exactly thirty-three pieces of toilet paper hiding and cry-
ing, hiding and crying, until they pull you out and take you home.

≈

AT ONE POINT on the hike, maybe three days in, I remember seeing trout hovering near my feet and legs in mountain rivers and
lakes. I remember seeing the backs and wingtops of birds. Never
had it occurred to me that looking at birds from a vantage point
above their flight changed the story. I saw a white-headed wood-
pecker, loons, bald eagles, and peregrine falcons. A northern gos-
hawk grazed my shoulder. I heard the sounds of boreal owls and a
great gray owl.

Nor had it occurred to me until that hike that the mountains
have ecological and biological communities, biomes. Alpine communities, forest, shrubland, and grassland communities, riparian
and wetland communities. The truth is this hike sat latent in my

body for many years, hidden underneath the great grand narrative of my failure and suffering, my mother's story and suffering, my sister's story and suffering, until later in life when I realized that trip had planted a seed in my body that perhaps my own identity was connected to something besides a biologic family.

I talked to several trees, especially when it occurred to me that I might not be able to make it all the way out, a thought I promised myself I'd die trying to avoid. Douglas firs and Engelmann spruce, ponderosa pines and aspens. I whispered secrets to the understory plants like elk sedge, lupines, sagebrush, and pine grass, hoping for solidarity.

I think I saw a mountain goat. On the fourth day I was close to hallucinating, so maybe I'm wrong, but I think that I did. I may have seen a black bear but can't be sure.

I saw my friend, this woman I loved, take such care teaching me how to put up and take down the tent, how to build the fire, how to cook food over it, how to clean myself and go to the bathroom and stay warm and inhabit the weather and terrain rather than fight it or fear it. Even with shredded feet.

I remember the smell of her skin from those days, a combination of campfire and sunscreen and organic balms she carried in little tins. The smell of her hair, captured by a bandanna sometimes, mountain air and lake water and campfire coffee. I remember watching every single finger of her right hand. I could likely draw you a picture. Her fingernails, the knuckles, the lines on her palms. Her eyes two blue pools I would associate with mountains for the rest of my life. Her smile and the lines around her eyes that were the evidence of a woman who smiles making their own topographies.

I don't remember how many days we hiked. Me in her flip-flop concoctions.

I don't remember the last climb down a steep face of mountain made from sharp jagged rocks the size of my kneecaps. I only remember being terrified I'd take a full frontal digger and wondering if they'd have to airlift me out, also wondering what I meant by "they." I do remember watching the Valkyrie run down that same terrain in another zigzag pattern. Yes, run. She was mountain goat beautiful. I think she started picking up the pace because she must have begun to worry I wouldn't be able to make it.

I do remember the land softened toward a forest, pine I think, at which point we were nearing a place where her perfect and good mother had left her truck to retrieve us. The trail at that point was flat and spongy. The Valkyrie ran ahead. She understood I was by then in a bit of a dangerous condition, so she *jogged the last few miles to the car. With her backpack on.* Every mile or so I'd find an arrow made of pebbles laid out for me on the trail pointing the way. When I found the first one I cried. I sat down on the ground. Every pebble arrow touched my heart. *Maybe this is love.* My gratitude had no language.

I knew the trail ended at a parking lot. Before I got there, I looked up and saw the Valkyrie running back—packless but smiling, laughing even—jogging like she'd just decided to get a bit of exercise. When she reached me, I crumpled. I don't know if that's actually true, but in my memory, I crumpled into a little heap there on the ground.

She came back to get me.

No one in my life, least of all any woman, had ever come back to get me, or save me, or coach me on how to run for my life, or teach me how to be stronger, though once my sister came home from college and asked me if I wanted to leave with her after my mother's first suicide attempt. I couldn't bring myself to leave my mother, so I said no. No one taught me what a period was, or sex, or cooking or cleaning or taking care of myself. No one taught me how to win races, or how to become an escape artist, or how to carry pain, or how to resist the pull to die. I made it up.

She may not have been a lesbian but my love for her was bigger than any body, without a language to account for it, without a story.

In fact, from this vantage point, what I remember is not that she was a woman at all, but that she was perfectly neither male nor female, but what I would call femascular, and that I suddenly wanted to find that in myself, in my own life; I wanted to make stories of figures who were not female or male, not hero or villain. I wanted to animate figures of mythic strength and beauty, not the beauty myth of my lifetime.

I shared my version of the story with the Valkyrie recently, decades since our hike. Here is what she said:

> Oh my, reality really depends on where you're standing, doesn't it! MY recollection of that trip was of the mighty warrior of you, trekking through the mountains with my undersized flip flops tied to your blister-covered feet, and of you expressing only appreciation and wonder. Zero complaints. And no mention from you of the fact that I was the one who thought that, instead of wearing your perfectly good tennis shoes, you should wear my mother's hiking boots, which clearly didn't fit and which gifted you with blisters within the first hours of our hike. So while your rec-

ollection is that I cared for you, mine is that I crippled you, and that you responded without accusation of any kind but only with appreciation for where you were and the moment we were having. I was in awe of how you could hold that toughness and tenderness within you without even noticing the miracle of that.

My story of myself dissolved, or at least shivered, shapeshifted for a nanosecond.

In her story, she crippled me—which is the word my mother carried in her body her entire life, a word I have carried in my own body like some kind of displaced allegiance . . . or love, and so seeing the word embedded in her story—that return, that echo, also shifted something around in me. The words crippled, toughness, and tenderness dislocate and open up into possibility in her telling.

What I'm telling you is that storytelling lets you *move*.

MIMIC

On the coast where I now live, on rainy days, when the trees, rivers, hills, and ocean all take on a kind of color between Payne's gray and moss green, my mind mists and drifts, and more often than not, I think of Olga, who loved rain as much as I do. Olga is the person who showed me how to go stand in the rain anytime I faced an ending. Olga taught me more about myself than any mother could, even though I only knew her a short time. Olga puffed up with steroids and anti-inflammatories making dough of her cheeks, burying a crooked smile that opened into a gap between her two front teeth. On rainy, thought-drifting days like these, I remember what it felt like to eat dinner at her table. I remember watching her cook all day, beginning sometimes the night before, her apron making a tent over her bulbous breasts and gut, her owl glasses too big for her head, her hair thinning and her cheeks flushed as the war between lupus and her spirit raged inside her.

I cry a little when I think of Olga, standing in the rain on my back deck. I can see the river, the edge of the ocean. My face carries salt not unlike the rain headed toward the river headed toward the ocean on the body of the world. Down the road, through the coast range, back into the city, the life I walked away from. Something is ending again.

My mother, unlike Olga, was a shit cook. She spent her days and nights selling houses, a born businesswoman. I too am a shit cook. I never learned when I went to college; I was only ever good at swimming. The year I first flunked out of college I broke my ankle. We—and the "we" was so very important at the time, a kind of communal identity of swimmers, one that I became exiled from—were running stadium steps before swim practice in the heat of West Texas. I hated running stadium steps passionately. Maybe that's why I turned my head to laugh at a joke my roommate made, and in that small turn of head and loss of focus, I caught my foot underneath a single stair. My body fell forward and my right foot and ankle did not. I heard a crack. Then pain. Then dizziness. I used to faint as a kid in the sun, so I could tell I was near passing out.

That broken ankle took me out of training. I was taken in a golf cart to the sports medicine clinic. The college campuses in Texas are vast. Walking back to my dorm took a long time no matter what the circumstances. I came out of the sports medicine complex with a cast up to my knee. I did not know I had begun a strange and complex journey away from myself to who I thought I was to find some bigger story.

As the days and nights of not swimming dragged on, I stopped going to my classes. I don't think I ever had a clear thought like, *stop going to classes.* I think I was just tired, and sad. Not about my training as a student-athlete. I already hated being a student-athlete, but the identity had gotten me out of my father's house, so when that chance came, I ran and never went back. I was sad because lying around in bed not doing anything felt better than anything I'd ever done in my life. Dreamy. Cocooned. Nothing pressing down. Nothing to hold in. Just a body in a bed with a cast. Just arms and legs not pounding the water. And so the sadness was about how something so obviously a failure could feel so good.

What I did mostly alone in my bed was draw. I loved drawing. I think I loved drawing more than any of the art majors I met. While I was filling drawing tablets with illustrations, I remembered that when I was five, I did not want to become a swimmer, or a writer, or a wife, or a mother, or a teacher, all things I would become later in life. When I was five, I wanted to be a painter. In bed with a broken ankle, I could feel my desire to be an artist in my fingers. Once I drew an image of the trees around my childhood home. I included our dog, Maggie, a pointer. I showed the drawing to my father the architect. He immediately began improving the shapes of the trees with a pencil. I suppose it was just his habit, but the gesture left its mark on me. A male authority coming in to improve my art. Alone in bed, my art was just my art, a reclamation it would take me decades to really believe in.

By the time summer came, I had not been a swimmer for long enough to never be a competitive swimmer again. Fifteen years of drive and ambition gone, swallowed up in an anticlimactic ending made from a broken bone. When I remembered why I became a swimmer in the first place, the clarity stunned me: my best friend was on the swim team at our community pool, so I followed her. I did what she did, I passed for someone who wanted to race and win.

I flunked out of college and, fitted with a walking cast after my initial cast, I landed in Boston to visit my sister, who was finishing graduate school at a prestigious university. I had nowhere else to go. My sister and I had both escaped our family and never looked back. Or more precisely, I hadn't yet the imagination to conjure a place to go.

There was nowhere at my sister's for me to stay, so my sister arranged for me to stay with her friend Olga, a poet who lived in a large old bohemian four-story house in Somerville.

The visit was meant to last a week or two, but my sister and I walked so hard and went so many places that I walked my cast to death. There was a lot going on in all that walking together. We'd been reunited in a way, suturing the wound of her leaving our family household when I was ten and she was eighteen. That gap between our ages and that decade alone with my father and mother took a toll on me. I had to fight my way out of that place. Siblings who survive abusive households know what it means to cleave, to fold back into each other, knowing the cleaving has left its marks. To this day my ankle aches. It never healed fully.

As it turned out, Olga had other tenants. Actually "tenant" is not the right word. Olga harbored other itinerant creatures. Cats, dogs, a hamster, a bird, a snake, an out-of-work American painter dropped from his New York City gallery for fucking too many underaged women, a Romanian concert pianist whose philandering husband had driven her to the brink of insanity, a refugee from Honduras without papers. It felt like the world had presented me with a door to another universe. I hobbled through it dim-witted but curious.

My visit turned into weeks. The cast eventually fell apart, and I found a job at a dress shop in Harvard Square. Nothing made any sense at all, which is why it felt so good to do it.

The Romanian concert pianist cried every time she played incredibly beautiful classical music on an incredibly terrible piano in the house. The refugee from Honduras went pantsless often. I don't know why. He wore large white underwear the entire summer he was there. He had an amazing smile with what seemed like too many teeth. We all moved around each other like animals. We didn't have conversations, we just sat down to eat Olga's dinners at night. I am certain conversations happened, but I was twenty, the age of not knowing how to listen yet.

On my lunch breaks from work I would go to Au Bon Pain, buy a fancy (to me) bread item, and eat it for lunch. Sometimes I ate on the quad where Harvard was nestled. I knew I was an outsider, especially in the rarified air of the Ivy League. I thought it was funny to eat lunch so near students. One day I followed some of them into a class and sat on the floor in the back of the lecture hall. I visited several classes in this manner. Because I didn't have to be a student, it was easy to receive the beauty of the lessons. I could walk in, walk out, then just go think about what I'd heard for as long as I wanted to. More often than not, I just sat on a bench and watched people. My favorite person was a woman in a trench coat with old-school cat-eye glasses who held a rolled-up newspaper and flapped it at anyone who came near. At first the woman was funny to me. I thought of her as "the flapper." Later on I came to admire her. But that burp in consciousness took years.

I confess with shame that Olga frightened me at first. Like so many people at twenty I didn't know anything about anything. I knew how to say yes when someone wanted to sleep with me, how to drink, how to read books I liked rather than books assigned to me, how to flunk out of college. I also had the bravado of a very young woman who had escaped her father and thus needed to assert her badassery upon anyone who would listen. It was just ex-hausting for most people, I can see now.

Olga frightened me because she rarely looked at me; she carried her own presence in a way that made me afraid to breathe. Ample and aging and dying, she didn't seem to care what clothes she wore. Or how she smelled—usually some combination of sweat, cumin, rosemary, Ivory soap, and skin that takes on place. Sometimes she wore the same clothes for days. In the kitchen, where I saw her the most, she was the absolute authority. She was the kitchen, and the kitchen was her. She was a poet and activist outside of her house. Mostly she scared me because she was dying from lupus. I kept my distance.

But Olga lured me closer, as she lured everyone, with the meals that she conjured, with the poems that she wrote, with an irrepress-ible "yes, but why?" no one could resist.

The day she finally looked at me, she pierced my skull open with her stare. Olga did not think I was a badass. Her eyes were the faint-est blue, so faint as to be almost transparent. Her cheeks puffed. She stirred a pot of lobster bisque. She didn't say anything. She just stared and stirred. Stared and stirred. But the stare got into me and turned into all kinds of things. *Do you intend to begin paying me any rent for your time here? I see you drawing all the time. Are you an art-ist? Do you want to be an artist? Will you go back to school? Are you a burden on your sister? Your sister works very hard. Your sister is bril-liant. Don't bother her too much. It took everything she had in her to leave. She left to save her own life. Do you know who you are yet? Taste this—no, don't tell me what you think, just taste it. I already know what I'm doing. You just look like someone who has not tasted.*

Olga's house was the color of blood. Maybe it wasn't, but in my memory, Olga's house carried meanings beyond the ordinary range of things. . . . Olga's house had a butterfly-shaped rash, raised red patches. Olga's house was sensitive to light. Ulcers lived under her house's mouth and nose. The bones of her house ached with arthritis and swelled. The lungs inflamed. Olga's house had seizures during windstorms. Nerve problems. Too much protein in the urine. My room in Olga's house was painted midnight blue. The room was small; there was a bunkbed. I slept on the bottom. At night I was afraid to use the bathroom for fear Olga might need it; there were no locks on any doors. She sometimes roamed the halls of the house at night in a white nightgown, moaning. Sometimes I peed in a water bottle and emptied it out of the bedroom window.

≈

THE DRESS SHOP in Harvard Square near Au Bon Pain aimed itself at women who were busy with on-the-go lives. The shoes were stylish but sensible. The skirts shaped for on-the-job, academic, or businesswoman. Mauve, navy, black, brown, the occasional burgundy. One section of the store was devoted to leotards, leggings, exercise and dancewear before yoga as an industry took over the country. Warm and stylish coats, thick-necked sweaters, all manner of hats for winter, umbrellas, casual dresses, fitted blazers.

I settled into being a woman worker in a Harvard Square dress shop remarkably quickly. I stopped wearing Doc Martens. I combed my hair. I wore plain skirts and sweaters. The work of helping women shop or folding and refolding clothes on a shelf or pressing them neat on a rack or working a register didn't bother me much. I could feel a rhythm, and inside this rhythm I didn't have to think. The monotony was like a hum I could live with. But everywhere comes with its difficulties. On occasion I had to clean the floor where a homeless woman had slid between the clothing racks to squat and pee. Or worse. This job likely influenced my slow but deepening understanding of the flapper. People in distress develop their own gestures, languages, codes for surviving a world intent on erasing them. I too would live a kind of ghost life when grief and trauma overtook me. I too would develop behaviors, gestures, codes for surviving. The dress shop had a specific clientele that was occasionally interrupted by those who did not fit in, just like Harvard with its ivy-covered walls.

In the evenings, after I walked home from work no matter the weather, I'd cloister myself in my little room in Olga's house and scan the newspaper listings for weddings, funerals, and especially art openings, any kind of event where there might be free food and alcohol within walking distance. I felt guilty that I didn't yet make enough money to pay Olga for rent, thus I felt guilty for eating her food. To be honest, even the meals scared me. I'd never eaten anything like them in my life. My mother cooked the kind of food that women from Texas cook. Or the kind of dinners patriarchal angry men require of their wives. Even after she went to work full-time as a Realtor, it was fried chicken, meat loaf, steak and potatoes. Spaghetti with Ragú sauce from a jar. Mostly I felt guilty because Olga was sick and dying and basically taking care of me and everyone around her.

As I look back, I can see I was sort of inverted or hapless with my wandering guilt and fear. I honestly had no idea how to be an adult in the world. No one had ever shown me. My older sister left when I was ten. My mother had entered the submerged existence of an alcoholic. My father was only good at architecture, rage bursts, molestation and domination of his daughter. I'm surprised I knew how to drive, but driving had been a necessity for going to and returning from swim team. I did not know how to cook or clean or dress or act in the world. I just mimicked other people. Luckily, I was good at it. Geminis are good at twinning.

I learned a great deal at the dress shop from the manager, Colette, and from my coworkers, Vicki and Angela, and from the women who came to buy clothes and shoes and leotards. I knew I wasn't anything *like* Colette or Vicki or Angela, but I could see plainly that they knew how to get around in the world as regular women. Colette was a born businesswoman. I joined her on her vintage furniture hunts through New England many times. Twice a year Colette would be invited to the owner's mansion for a celebration of some sort, and she'd talk about it for days. So I could see Colette wanted up. Vicki was absolutely from a working-class origin, with a Boston accent thick enough to pronounce "car" *cah*. But her rise was happening quickly due to her boyfriend being from a wealthy family. I could tell from the small shifts in her jewelry, her nails, her hair, her mascara—which went from grocery store clumpy to Estée Lauder to brands you could not find except in rich-lady spas. Money was transforming her into a higher form of feminine. I could tell she secretly wanted to be manager, but I could also tell she wanted to be elevated by marriage away from working altogether. Angela was Italian, her dark eyes as fierce as her laugh. I don't think she trusted me for a moment that I knew her. I think she knew I wasn't real from the get-go. Angela suffered no fools. Her husband was a construction worker and they weren't leaving the solid ground of family loyalty in a Boston suburb. Fuckin' A.

Colette and I hit it off. I'm not sure why. I may have been so deeply performing a self that I appeared falsely interesting with my west coast vibe. Or she may have been lonely for someone to match her quick wit and intelligence. Or maybe she could sense the former competitor in me. More likely it was none of those things. Most likely I simply knew how to successfully mimic her back to her in a way that made her feel seen. Colette was driven and ambitious. I knew she was going to succeed. I just had no idea what that meant. That drive and ambition had fizzled in me. The closest thing I had to a sense of self was when I stood near someone who had it, even the flapper. The flapper vibrated with energy like a hummingbird. This mesmerized me.

Colette radiated the light of a person on the move. Her light and energy moved me. Also, I could match her beer for beer, and outdrink her when it came to hard liquor. Which may have been my appeal. Drinking looks badass on a young woman to another young woman, until it doesn't.

Once we sat on her roof with beers and a spliff. She asked me what I wanted to do with my life. She seemed pretty sure about hers. I mean, do you have any interest in being the head of one of the departments, she wanted to know. There are departments? Yeah, she said, like the swimwear and exercise area—you could be in charge of that. You know, because of your swimming background. You're a natural.

I sucked on the joint and stared at the tops of other houses. My chest got tight and cold. This question was completely foreign to me. What in the world was happening? I didn't know anything about anything.

For more money, she said. And then there's assistant manager . . . you'd be a natural at that, too.

I'd be lying if I said this occurred to me at the time, but the seed of it did: *If you keep moving in this direction on this path you will become a Colette.* At the time, on the roof, sucking in weed, drinking beer, I thought something like *Fuck.*

Later that night, maybe because I was still a little high, I sat down in Olga's kitchen. We were alone. She sliced onions quickly and without looking and hummed something underneath her breath. Not exactly a tune. She then sliced up two carrots, two pieces of celery, mushrooms. She carefully stripped the sticks of thyme from her garden and chopped them up, too. Chicken was already browning in a big pan. Minced fresh garlic sat waiting. Bacon dripped its fat on a plate covered in a paper towel. She brought me a glass of water without speaking, also without missing a beat of chopping or stirring. She looked dreamy, beautiful. For the first time in ever, I asked her what she was making.

She didn't answer. Her hum increased in volume.

I felt puny and stupid but not ashamed. The kitchen was warm and I wasn't bothering anyone, not even her.

You should go sit for John, she said without looking at me.

I sat drinking my glass of water.

When I finished my water, I stood up to leave. I took one of the biggest breaths of my life—just trying to breathe in everything good of that moment, the smell of chicken fat and bacon and thyme, the warmth from the stove, the trace of my high not yet gone, the red of the walls, the other herbs hanging upside down with dried flowers in the window, rosemary, sage, little scarlet peppers, roses with their dried-up heads hanging down, three of John's paintings on the walls, one of Olga looking like a white woman Buddha, two other nudes, the old dog underneath the table, which I finally noticed was some kind of Australian shepherd mix, one of its eyes brown, one blue, and the organic mound that was Olga in the middle of all of it.

I was already climbing the stairs to my room when I heard her say, "Coq au vin."

What I wouldn't recall until years later is that I had watched every move she made to create coq au vin. And every meal she made for the rest of that year. Lobster bisque. Mushroom and spinach lasagna. Kota psiti. Pesto-stuffed trout. Chicken mole and chili. A quiche. A soufflé. Rack of lamb. Braised salmon. I'm still a shit cook. But her cooking got into my body. When called upon, I can make a meal. My body remembers things I do not.

The next day I went to sit for John.

John's studio looked exactly like my secret internal dreamscape, exactly like the erotic fantasy I had imagined while I was in bed with a broken ankle. I'd seen photographs of famous painters' studios. Willem de Kooning's. Francis Bacon's. Joan Mitchell's. Lee Krasner's. Jackson Pollock's. What I admired and yearned for the most was the mess of colors, textures, various areas in disarray, a work of art at the center coming to life. The smell of oils and turpentine and linseed oil. The rows of brushes jutting up from old jars. The patches and drips and smears of color—every color imaginable—threatening to overtake the room and everything in it. The piles of bones or feathers or rocks or paper or dead insects or shells collected in corners on purpose.

John's studio was in an old warehouse. John turned on the shitty little portable space heater. He was seventy. I know this because Olga once made him a red velvet cake with the number *70* in rose petals on white buttercream frosting.

When I took off my clothes and situated myself on some old ki-

lim pillows and he sat down in front of a canvas and easel, I felt like
we were an archetype of a genius artist and a nymph or muse. The
reason I knew exactly what to do was that I was a young woman,
and so taking one's clothes off with any man was not anything dramatic to me, and I had already been a life model to help pay for
college, back when I attended college. I did not know how to be a
woman in the world, but I knew how to be an object without thinking or feeling, first bred into me from my father. Entering the story
was familiar to me.

John painted for around four hours. After about three hours, I
said I was cold, so he brought me a turquoise shawl. I said thank
you. He gently fondled me for about twenty minutes. He sucked on
one nipple. He fingered my wet. He humped my hip. He unbuttoned his pants and held himself. I held my pose. I didn't think
anything. I didn't feel anything. Nothing unusual was happening
to me. He made a sound I'd never heard before, soft, like an animal
in the garden sunning itself. Then he went back to his painting.

John was Olga's husband. She'd simply moved him to the lower
bedroom at some point in their lives, and so they lived apart and
together in the same house.

I never spoke of the fondling to anyone. In those days, the
moment came and went without weight. That's what I thought at
the time.

But I left Olga's house about a week after.

I didn't have much to pack up in my leaving, just the original
clothes of a person who thought she was visiting her sister for a few
weeks, and some clothes from the dress shop that looked like they
belonged to someone named Colette. My plan was to simply walk
downstairs and out the door without notice of any sort. My plan

was to leave three months' worth of rent on the kitchen table; three months' worth was all I had managed to save. I'd scrawled *Thank You for Everything* on a scrap of white paper, and my plan was to leave that on the kitchen table as well.

The kitchen was empty—to my great relief; although the day I chose to leave, the room was also full with the smell of blueberry muffins with walnuts. I wanted one. I hunted for them but could not find them. I left my money and my note. I turned to leave. The dog padded toward me and brushed against my shin, then walked on. The cat stared at me from a sunny window ledge, indifferent. The snake didn't move. It might have been dead. When had that happened? The walls of the house were silent and held their pose. I walked out the front door, a deep blue door with chipped paint and animal scratches on it, closing it behind me, then I closed the crappy screen door. I was halfway down the walkway overgrown with grass and weeds and wildflowers when Olga came around from the side of the house. She lumbered over to me. I thought she carried some kind of basket for collecting herbs or flowers or vegetables. But that is not what she carried.

Take these, she said.

A large flat box. Once she opened it in front of me, I saw it was filled with oil paints, a variety of brushes.

Before I could say anything, the sky opened up. Olga closed the box up, pushed it toward me, and looked straight skyward. Her glasses catching raindrops. Her flushed cheeks. Her hair immediately matted to her skull. Her dress—the one she'd been wearing for weeks—was not zipped up in the back and hung slightly forward off her shoulders. She wore two different galoshes. One black. One red.

Like a moron, I held the flat box over my head to shield myself from the downpour, or I tried to, but Olga stopped me.

No, no. Look up. There is nothing more perfect in the world than rain. Every time it rains, go stand in it, and mark what is ending.

I hadn't a clue what she meant by that. Her glasses fogged up, but I could see when she pointed her face to the sky again that her eyes were closed. Her whole body looked to be saying *Thank you. Thank you. Thank you.*

I went to my sister's tiny attic apartment that day. She took me in. We went to eat tuna salad sandwiches from our favorite deli. We got the worst food poisoning I've ever had in my life, and we spent the next week retching and crawling up the terrible ladder stairs to the bathroom. Like passing through a birth canal together. Twinning imperfectly.

Later, my sister and I got an apartment together. She finished her dissertation. I left to go live with my boyfriend back in Texas, one of the worst mistakes I ever made in my life. I don't know if I was a burden to my sister when she was trying to finish her PhD, but I suspect that I was. Terribly. And I'd do it again, later in life, when my own life exploded again. Reaching for an other because I couldn't find a self. I don't know if Colette thought we were twinning. If my leaving hurt her. I don't know if John even saw me as a person. He kept painting. Olga died of lupus. My sister became a professor of literature for many years. Her dissertation adviser was a famous poet, also a philandering schmo. He too is dead now. I did not take Olga's gift—John's paints—with me.

Once when I stayed there I bumped into Olga in the middle of the night in the kitchen. I meant to get some water. She just stood there in the moonlight in her big white tent nightgown. Her skin glowed like a pearl. She turned the light on. Make me an egg, will you. She sat down at the kitchen table.

Is she sleepwalking? I made her an egg. Or tried to. It stuck to the pan. Wrong pan. Not enough butter. Heat too high. It was the ugliest, most pathetic egg ever. She came and looked at it smeared and seared sadly there in the pan. That's not an egg, she said, and left the kitchen and climbed the stairs.

≈

I DID NOT PAINT anything anywhere after I left Olga's house. For forty years. I swallowed my desire to be an artist like an ugly fried egg. Does it matter where the endings are, where the beginnings?

Content, if you want to say, is a glimpse of something, an encounter, you know, like a flash—it's very tiny—very tiny. Content. Willem de Kooning said that.

I am now the age Olga was when she died from lupus. The age my mother was when she died of breast cancer. Last year I left my life as a teacher, a writer, a community builder, a literary activist to come live near the ocean. Quietly. I am inside some kind of ending, even if I don't quite know how to name it. I have no idea how long it will last. There are extraordinary trees here: Sitka spruce and alders. A good dog named Sadie. Eagles. Blue herons and egrets. Hummingbirds, a ride-or-die husband of twenty years, black bears, deer, hawks, rabbits, barred owls and spotted owls, cougars, and more elk than I've ever seen in my life, or ever will. I am standing in the rain on my back porch. I close my eyes and point my face toward the sky. *Thank you.*

Inside, a canvas waits for me to become something of my own making, paints in a beautiful box at my feet.

SKYDIVER:

ONE

*P*eople are sometimes too interested in "what happened"—the plod of plot and action. Sometimes the rest of the story, or perhaps the heart of the story, is carried by image, repetition, tiny intensities not captured fully from plot and action. A very intense drama played out in my relationship with Devin. You will not find it on these pages. The drama is not the story, or, the story of why and how relationships dissolve or crescendo is every story, living inside all of us to differing degrees, rising and falling in waves. When I focus on moments, on small intensities that may or may not interest anyone else, I'm reminding us how those tiny pieces of a life are sometimes carrying bigger meanings than the big, dull, thunderous calamities that befall us all.

If I track not just plot and action, but impressions, emotional intensities, associations, repetitions, images, can I transmogrify and reframe the story?

What "happened" is Devin and I loved each other into the death of our marriage, which is not any kind of unique story. Oceans of women have fallen for dangerous men, or angry men, or depressed men, or death-driven men. Legions of marriages fail.

I don't want to write about the plot of what happened to him.

I want to find the heart of the story underneath that.

≈

52-YEAR-OLD CAUCASIAN MALE, reportedly found within a pit adjacent to a crane that he apparently fell from while climbing the tower, approximately 80 feet.

Multiple external and internal traumatic injuries.

See toxicology report: elevated levels of alcohol; acute alcohol intoxication.

Tattoos include "Carpe Diem," "Don't Try," "Unaffiliated," and "Artistic Disorder," as well as the Chinese symbol for longevity.

The case report lists his death as Accident/Suicide.

What a narrative space between accident and suicide.

The accident report says that he said that night he was going for a walk. I already knew Devin had a history of suicidal ideation. I already knew he had been to rehab and detox, which entered the narrative of the report, too. According to the report, he had just climbed the same tower on New Year's Day.

I know Devin climbed various towers in Alabama in his late teens and early twenties before I met him. He told me the stories.

I do want to write about his death, but not the one that has been so carefully and terribly documented.

I want to revision his story away from that idiotic obituary, away from the accident report and autopsy. I want to write him back to life, even if it kills me, an impossible story. Or I want to write open a space where what he loved lives, which in the end, was not me, even if it was, briefly. I understand now that love is always the fall.

Devin loved his father, who left his mother when he was a boy, a man who drank too much and sometimes jumped out of planes. Sky diver.

Devin loved drinking.

Devin loved the I Ching.

Devin loved the poetry of Charles Bukowski and the music of Jim Morrison, the Red Hot Chili Peppers, Nirvana, and the Black Crowes.

Devin loved Butoh theater.

Devin loved—or became obsessed with, which may be what love is for an artist—drawing and painting abstract disfigured faces.

I know why Devin loved his father. He loved and followed his father for the same reasons that Icarus did. Once Devin told me a story about going with his father on a jump. Though he was not old enough to jump as a child, a child with hair that fell in waves as black as space, a child with shoulder blades jut-cut like a bird at his back and a rib cage that swelled with the uncontainable imagination of a boy thrumming his chest, he would go with his father.

He'd watch his father zip up his silver flight suit and tighten the straps of his parachute and secure his helmet and goggles. Just before the leap into nothingness his father would turn to him, give him a thumbs-up, and say, "You only live once!" Devin would then watch his father jump into nothing, quietly counting in his head, *one two three*, to calm himself. And Devin would be left standing between earth and sky, the sky pulling toward space and the earth pulling toward ground, like he was the small beating heart and guts between, the only thing connecting anything to anything, the only thing keeping everything from falling apart.

And then his father would be gone, just like when his father left Devin's mother when they divorced, and Devin would be left standing between earth and sky, the sky pulling toward space and the earth pulling toward ground, like he was the small beating heart and guts between, the only thing connecting anything to anything, the only thing keeping everything from falling apart.

I remember thinking how hard it is for a boy like that to keep from falling. To hold on.

Devin told me up there, fatherless, at the mouth of the plane door, that's when he'd begin to shake. He told me he always stood too close to the airplane's wide-open mouth of a door and he never felt secured enough like a boy his age should be. He'd hold on to some straps, thwapping in the high wind, his hair a storm on his head.

And he told me he would wonder, would his father's body float perfectly to the ground, safe and sound? Or would it be crushed into a thousand star shards on the surface of the earth?

Later, back on the ground, his father would slap him round the shoulders and pull him into his body and say, "We lived another day, god damn it, didn't we just?" And he'd crack open a Coors Light to celebrate.

Devin told me that when he was on the plane in the sky, he'd stand at the open door shaking, and he'd close his eyes and hold his breath and let go of the straps he was clutching for dear life after his father leapt.

He'd whisper,

One

Two

Three

The voice of a boy.

That's how he'd get his breathing to go back into his chest like a normal person instead of a light-as-air boy standing too close to the edge of the world, a father gone to flight or atmospheric drift or wherever fathers go to be gone. Devin would open his eyes and scan the skies for a speck of a man with an orange parachute.

Even after Devin was an adult, in moments that felt like the edge of something, he'd repeat *one two three,* after lovers and marriages and affairs and dramatic breakups and dismal divorces, after arguments and binges and violations and violences, after addictions, after incarcerations, after returns and rejections and resolutions and ruin, after all the great leaps and the terrible dives that make up a life, he'd say out loud to no one in particular, like an inside joke, or the opposite of prayer, or the sounds humans make when they are afraid to do something difficult or banal:

one

two

three

The beautiful leap or fall unended, forever suspended; winged.

I know how storytelling holds us.

I know why Devin loved to drink. I know why we met each other in that ocean called alcohol. Suspend the story before it swallows us.

I know why he loved the poetry of Charles Bukowski and the music of Jim Morrison, because I have now met many men who carry synchronistic attachments to them as larger-than-life figures, often extraordinarily creative men with absent fathers.

I know how to read the faces he painted.

Each line, each brushstroke, goes into my body like a second language. A blur reads like that liminal place between us we rarely inhabited but longed for, like when we were kiss-close and boundaries dissolved, but still left us lost. Love didn't help. A jagged burst or crooked scratch reads to me like a code for *I want in, I want out, I am alive, I am dead, this is the precipice of my face.*

And I know why he loved Butoh theater so much. The faces he drew and painted seemed to stand in for all the things he wanted to say or feel about his own identity. He loved the way Butoh faces were like death masks, or deranged beauty. But what I know scares me.

≈

MOST HISTORIES of Butoh theater begin by describing the form as Japanese dance theater, movement, performance. Most histories also mention how the art form followed World War II, rising in 1959 through the collaboration of its founders Kazuo Ohno and Tatsumi Hijikata. From there, a wide array of language is used to describe the core emotions and concepts around Butoh theater practices, including but not limited to: performing physical and emotional distress, gestures that are grotesque, playful, taboo, extreme, absurd, sexually graphic.

Devin's interest was not so much in the history of the form but in the aesthetics of "the squat, earthbound physique," the natural movements of regular people, the crude physicality and rude gestures, the visceral and embodied sexual excess and closeness-to-death imagery, decay, a kind of violent dance between creation and destruction. The grimacing faces blurring the line between life and death, beauty and horror. The emphasis on bringing humanity back to primal, elemental forces in some liminal space between pleasure and pain. I know because I watched his face.

He was interested in Butoh-Kaden, the world of bird and beast.

Crow on the road, thick bills, shiny black feathers, round back, the caw.

The stretch of a crow's neck.

Crow in the snow, perched, shivering, protruding breast, pecking.

I can still hear him reading to me about the crow in Butoh, with the echo of his last name following me forever: "A crowd of the dead sent to hell. Extreme hunger. Food turns into smoke as soon as it is brought to the mouth. Desperate ghosts. Assimilate materials, dry and slightly distinguished from each other." Gather as crow. Somehow the lines got into my body the way poetry does, by amplifying affect and bypassing sense, grammar, the plod and plot of regular sentences. I remember the night he read those lines to me and then performed "crow" naked and drunk in front of me while I wrapped myself up in the covers of our bed. He was good at it. His black hair. His black eyes. His arms suspended. His legs in a twitch-walk. His head jerking here, then there. I was high. I was so in love the love swallowed me whole. It took almost nothing for me to believe he was an actual crow. When we fucked later, I closed my eyes and I saw a million black and blue feathers.

One night before I fell asleep he asked me, do you think a face could be a crow? I thought about that question all night. I took it into our lives. His question haunted me.

I remember the day he first read to me about Yoshiyuku Takada. A modern performance group, Sankai Juku, founded by Ushio Amagatsu in 1975, brought a series of Butoh performances to America in 1984. He read aloud to me the passages that described what happened to Yoshiyuku Takada.* My face got hot. I was holding a secret.

On September 10, 1985, the Sankai Juku dance company performed Butoh in Pioneer Square in Seattle, Washington. The dancers hung from a building upside down from ropes tied to their ankles, a gesture meant to metaphorize life and death. A minute or so after the dance began, the rope holding performer Yoshiyuku Takada broke. He fell six stories—eighty feet—to his death.

During his fall, he did not flail or scream, and when he hit the pavement, his body makeup—the traditional white, in this case, covered in flour—"sent up a small puff of powder into the air."

The crowd assembled screamed and gasped and then went silent. Some embraced. Others cried. Many who were there at the time say they carry the memory of his fall and his body hitting the ground in their own bodies, that they are haunted by the fall.

The performance was titled *Jomon Sho*, or Homage to Prehistory, subtitled "Dance of Life and Death."

I stayed very quiet, listening to Devin tell me what I already knew.

---

* See Alan Stein, "Sankai Juku Dancer Yoshiyuku Takada Dies After Falling Five Stories During a Performance in Seattle's Pioneer Square on September 10, 1985," HistoryLink .org, September 5, 2012, " historylink.org/File/10167.

≈

I WAS IN A BAR across the street that day. In Seattle. I was twenty-two. We would not meet for some years. It's just a memory I carry. When Devin read to me about the event, I didn't say anything because I was afraid. It felt like I brought some terrible fall to him that mesmerized him—two realities, one real, one imagined, colliding.

I remember how moved he was by the story, moved to tears, moved to drinking all night, all week, how he dreamed of him, how he wrote about him, how he painted about him, how he was haunted by this man's story. That's how artists take what moves them in the world into their lives and bodies.

I fell for Devin the way he fell for him. The beauty of the fall.*

≈

I WAS NOT STUDYING Butoh theater, but as I look back, I can see that I too was moving deathward—my passions were women artists on some kind of edge, like Marguerite Duras, Kathy Acker, Virginia Woolf, or death-driven friends like Anne Sexton and Sylvia Plath—how they drank each other in. I had a scotch in one hand and rocks in my pocket. Devin looked so beautiful to me. I already carried a beautiful death in my body, my baby daughter. If the journey was unto death, I was ready. Or so I thought.

But then more and more books happened to me, and something ignited in me that was not Devin's death drive, but something else,

---

* In his breathtaking book *What Is the Grass* Mark Doty often captures the intimate space between love and death: "You need to both remember where love leads and love anyway; you can both see the end of desire and be consumed by it all at once. The ecstatic body's a place to feel timelessness and to hear, ear held close to the chest of another, the wind that blows in there, hurrying us ahead and away, and to understand that this awareness does not put an end to longing but lends to it a shadow that is, in the late hour, beautiful."

and our stories began to pull apart. From this distance, I can see the fractals of our lives splitting off in different directions like the arborization of dendrites. For Devin, death was still beautiful, more beautiful than me by far. For me, death was alchemizing, a space of generative possibility.

I'm not sure there is any other way to say this: lines I read in books written by women became larger than my love—which was like a gap, a cavern, some irrecoverable space between us. I birthed my own imagination, which in turn birthed my solitude. More and more writing came out of me. I wrote these lines from Marguerite Duras with a purple Sharpie on the wall of our bedroom, like some giant magical message I found in a bottle. I couldn't help it:

> *The person who writes books must always be enveloped by a separation from others. That is one kind of solitude. It is the solitude of the author, of writing. To begin with, one must ask oneself what the silence surrounding one is—with practically every step one takes in a house, at every moment of the day, in every kind of light, whether light from outside or from lamps lit in daytime. This real, corporeal solitude becomes the inviolable silence of writing. I've never spoken of this to anyone. By the time of my first solitude, I had already discovered that what I had to do was write.*

Devin said, staring at my wall scroll, "In the I Ching, no blame. A place of transition has been reached. Free choice can enter." We laughed. We fucked. Were we speaking to each other in code all those years? A line, an image, a performance moment, a drawing, one story at a time?

My growing solitude—my hunger for aloneness that was just

getting born in me—did not serve our story well. The life force emerging in me wrecked the plot of us.

≈

I HAVE A BLACK BOOK. I call it the Book of Devin. At the end of our marriage, Devin traveled away from me to France and carried the black sketchbook with him. He filled it with sketches and writing. Upon his return, amidst the demise of our marriage, he mailed it to me.

I have ten thousand feelings about the contents of the Book of Devin, even about the book as an object when I hold it, the hard black cover, the insides vibrating. Besides the countless sketches and poems and entries, one page haunts me like no other.

> *I don't know what to do, Lidia. I think I must for the first time in my life be honest with everyone. You know I love you. I will never love again like the way we loved. We are always in each other's heads and hearts—marked. No matter what. Yes. I love Christy. I think she may be pregnant with my child. My second child in the world. If so I will be a father. Nothing scares me more. Now. I've fallen in love with a woman in Paris named Audrey—23—heroin addict, valium addict, when she opens her eyes in the morning the first thing she does is reach for her purse—1 valium and a cigarette—just to wake up. I don't know what to do. I don't know what decisions to make. My life is a mess—but that is another story—a boring one. I think you are the only person in the world I trust completely. And you know that you know me better than anyone. Any advice? Hahahahaha. I've made this mess. I know. But I don't know what to do. I simply don't know. I know this will hurt you. But I think I must be honest. With me. With you.*

With Christy. With Audrey. I'm so tired of lies. I hate myself because of them. If you please I will continue a bit more. I have a new tattoo. On my ring finger. Audrey has the same. We got them together. Our relationship is not about sex. In fact, we had sex only one time. We ate too many valium, wine, ecstasy, etc. . . . I don't even remember if I came. She is an artist. This is not bad. She is lost. She doesn't speak to her parents. She became addicted to heroin at sixteen. Her parents put her in a psych hospital. She hates them. Her only boyfriend—Thomas— died of an overdose. Only 20 years old. She has been clean for about a year except for 4 days about 2 weeks before I came along. Binger. Her hands shake. She is asthmatic. She smokes 3 packs of cigarettes a day. She is very pretty. I fell in love. She wants me to come live in Paris. I don't think so. She is too different. Very nervous. Jealous. Addicted. I love her because she is you at 23. I don't want to hurt you. I want to be honest for the first time in my life.

FOR MANY YEARS, I could not read the Book of Devin without breaking down or throwing up. And yet I'd look at it. After he died, I put the book in a drawer. I could not open it. But the trace of everything I felt kept showing up on my body—like a rash from nowhere, or a pain in my spine or neck or hip, or scar tissue. Non-sensical words like lucid dreaming at odd times during the day or night: No one is ever again going to say those kinds of things to me again love language is death language no one is ever again going to mail me a book like they pulled out their own heart put it in an envelope sent it sailing across oceans and time to the one person they thought could carry it sometimes I'm scared it's my fault he's dead what if I had stayed with him through more crucibles as bad as it got as much as he hurt me even once pointing a gun at me and asking me to stop loving him and sleeping with other women and drinking to oblivion and the words he said the most awful words that only people who love each other so much they could die would ever say to each other don't we make those promises to have and to hold in sickness and in death or is it health who means them why what if I could have helped him to stop drinking to heal I now know about myself I can take a great deal of punishment which I knew as a child internalized as an adult why didn't I just take it isn't that what I'm good at what if he was reaching out trusting that I'd catch him right when I walked away and made a boundary so that I could save myself what if it was my love that killed him because I left how many women have endured loving men who hurt them was that the story I was supposed to endure am I a monster for choosing a self a life stepping into a different story am I a monster am I a monster?

I don't know what to do with words like that so I do what I do know how to do. I throw them into stories; I watch them move and I can walk again.

MOTHER

A tiny hummingbird's nest sits on my bloodred writing desk. The nest was a gift, and yet every time I look at it I ask myself, what happened to the hummingbirds? Were they finished with the small home? Were they displaced? Did the nest fall when the hummingbirds left, or was the nest invaded? Did some other creature kill them and eat them? Or is the absence marked by flight and becoming? Was it death or life?

It's a question that haunts me even as the nest-gift is filled with aura to me. I am a lover of solitary objects, particularly organic objects: bones, hair, nests, animal skulls, feathers, rocks, shells, petals. Everything of life that it once held, the tiny hearts beating, the small wings fluttering, the hovering of it all, now untraceable but for bits of minuscule feather fluff woven here and there into a cup along with plant down, bark, lichen, leaf matter, and spider silk. The empty nest is either a delicate and beautiful artifact from the natural world or it is a stain, a violence.

The emptiness.

Hummingbirds select sheltered locations for building nests. Dense or thorny shrubs. The forked branch of a tree. The locations that intrigue me the most include those balanced on wires or Christmas holiday lights. On top of porch lamps or security cameras. Inside basketball nets, on top of wind chimes, ceiling sprinklers, the very top of a cactus. What formidable imaginations—to choose such unusual shelter spots. The nests are built solely by the female bird. She chooses the nesting sites, gathers the materials, raises the babies. She spends several hours a day for seven days collecting materials in a kind of frenzy.

Then she does something unusual.

She holds still.

In the fall of 2019 I was the writer in residence at a college in rural upstate New York. The job involved nine months on-site where I taught one creative writing seminar two days a week.

The rest of the time was mine.

That sentence had never happened to me before in my life.

The gift of alone. For nine months.

≈

WHEN I SAY ALONE, what I mean is, my husband stayed home in Oregon that year to help our son make the transition from high school to college. Had I stayed home that year with them, I would have had to face my son's leaving for college, too.

I am not lying when I say I thought it might kill me. I started fearing and talking to anyone who would listen about my dread and sadness about my son leaving home to go to college. No really, ask around. There are probably people who will read this who remember how many years I talked about my son's pending departure. I'd cry talking about it. Many women and men were compassionate, they'd put their hands on my shoulders and ask, "When does your son leave for college?" And I'd have to confess, "In five years." Or four. Or three. Or two. Then one. They'd look at me with concern or something like pity. Who does that? Mourns the loss before it even happens?

I'll tell you who. I was mourning my son's leaving before it ever happened because I carry loss inside my chest where a heart should be. My body is a lifedeath space. *Lily.* So instead of withstanding the moment of my son's leaving, I moved into that beautiful writer house provided by an esteemed private college over two thousand miles away.

I understand the depth of privilege this opportunity afforded me, even though nothing like this had ever happened to me in my life until that moment; my jam prior to this gig was teaching at a community college for eighteen years, teaching in correctional facilities, and then founding a writing space for people who can't go to college at all. I know how lucky I have been. Boo-hoo, you scored a visiting writer job and your son ascended to college seemingly effortlessly.

Ascensions.

Perhaps because I was raised Catholic for a while growing up, or perhaps because I've spent my entire adult life-force endeavoring to help people who get shoved to the margins grow wings, the first thing I felt was irrepressible guilt; a sticky, thick, and putrid guilt that oozes like too-old blood that got stuck in some mother-daughter wound.

I puzzled on that guilt. Should I turn this job down? Money and time, two things I only knew how to scrap for. Wasn't the scrap and hustle more important than the opportunity? Wasn't I just another white woman jackass if I took this opportunity? Then I realized my ego was doing some kind of slippery dance. Fuck that, I thought. Guilt is useless and just another tricky form of privilege. Quit having false fluttery frenzied battles with yourself and suck it up. This chance won't come again. Ever. You are not more righteous if you are in love with your own scrap and struggle than you are with your own possibility.

The next emotion I felt was unworthiness. It is not a lie to say I know hundreds of writers who are more talented than I am, whose work lifts me and keeps me from giving up, or in, every day of my life. Some of them are famous. Some are not. Some have yet to publish. None of that matters. What matters is the fact of their words coming alive on pages in spite of the world. The heart and art of them. So I thought to myself, get the fuck over yourself. Honor all of those writers you love by being present inside the great storytelling rivers that lead to an ocean bigger than all of us. Step up, woman. Hold the space for whoever comes next. And do what you always do when you are let in a door of privilege: move over and share the space with other writers you love; see how you can inspire youngsters to *Fuck. Shit. Up.*

That's how I came to embrace the alone.

On the first night of my sojourn in a house not mine, I took off my clothes, turned off all the lights, and took the hottest bath of my life, the only light from the bathroom window, like an eye directly on the moon.

Inside the alone, a grief bird freed herself.

Never let anyone tell you your grief is an emptiness.

There is an alone inside grief, and it is yours, and the alone is both unbearable and simultaneously beautiful. Never let anyone tell you how long your grief should last, or what to do with it.

I have spent whole decades inside grief.

I have spent whole decades inside an alone, whether or not there were any people around.

Sometimes inside the alone a story emerges.

In this story there was a grief bird girl, maybe with a red head and a black mask, her body gray and white.

Inside this alone story there was a woman with one wing for an arm. The wing was gray and missing some important feathers. The wing was heavy with age and flight. Due to the wing, the woman had only been able to use one of her arms, one of her hands, to write.

When I say my grief lifted, I mean that it grew wings and took flight, exactly like a tiny fierce hummingbird leaving a nest.

Night.

Water.

Moon.

Window.

Bird.

Body.

Write.

Our bathtub at home sucked and our water didn't ever get hot, just like every other house or apartment I've inhabited. We lived in an old Craftsman-style house in the shitty end of not-quite-Portland . . . something was always breaking down or rusting away or just not quite working right, but the house is filled with love and art so who gives a fuck?

This endless hot water and a functioning bathtub—this was an *epic* moment for me. Plus, the bathroom was bigger than some apartments I lived in. Sitting in the bathtub alone in the house in the dark the first night, an unusual feeling came forward and filled my entire body. One I had not prepared for. Eyes closed. Hot water all around my body. Tub like a perfect porcelain cup around me. The comfort and ease of darkness and peoplelessness only available inside a deep, dark, perfect alone. Which is how it occurred to me.

My pleasure.

The pleasure of a woman whose children—one who died, one who grew—are gone, a woman whose blood has come back to her forever.

I put my hand to the other mouth of me there in the water. I parted the lips of a self. With one finger two fingers I entered myself, the cave of my being, the lifedeath space. With my heavy wing hand, I pounded my clit. The water became waves. My body the waves. My eyes were closed but I recognized the heat surge of my "I" rising in my hips and cunt.

At the moment of my "I" coming, I heard a bird outside, a bird with a red head and a black mask and a gray and white breast, and the moon was there and she swallowed the bird into her.

After that I had two arms, two hands.

At the end of the nine mine-alone months, I returned home. My son returned home from college, too, because of Covid. So the cleaving was softened. I am not ashamed to admit his coming home elated me, though I tried to act casual around it, I tried not to hover too near every nanosecond, I tried not to flutter my heart against his so hard I left a bruise or a stain.

I tried to hold still.

My husband said the hardest aspect about our being gone was

the emptiness of the house, and how his heart felt away from his body.

One day when my son and I went for a walk through the neighborhood—I bet we all came to know our own neighborhoods more intimately than ever before during those two years—I saw a frenzied blur out of the corner of my eye.

A white hummingbird. Leucistic, not albino, because its eyes, feet, and bill were black. I pulled that universal parent move where I threw my arm against Miles's chest to stop him, even though he is over six feet tall. I pointed to the bird. I could hear us breathing against our Covid masks one second two seconds three seconds— and then the hummingbird was gone.

My son said, I think I just felt awe. Was that awe?

Annie Leibovitz said in her phenomenal book *Pilgrimage* that watching her children stand mesmerized over Niagara Falls was an exercise in renewal at a not great time in her life. "It taught me to see again," she said.

Each year hummingbirds travel on two migrations. One north, one south. The migrations can span thousands of miles. During migrations across the Gulf of Mexico, they can fly up to five hundred miles. Hummingbirds can fly on every axis. Research indicates that hummingbirds can travel as much as twenty-three miles in one day.

They beat their wings up to eighty times a second, which creates the soft humming sound.

I think the nest on my desk carries the trace of a mother's labor.

I think the emptiness carries the fullness of her life, how she has to keep moving in order to become, how her erotic power and creativity return to her, how she can bring them back to life with her hands.

I think the emptiness of the nest is like my mother-gut, that space that held grief and death and life and joy, now filled with laughter and fat and bulging with stories.

MONSTER

The movie *Creature from the Black Lagoon* was made in 1954, before I was born. As a kid, I loved this movie so much I used to cry hysterically at the end when the creature is killed. I didn't give a shit about the woman victim or anyone killed by the creature—like all idiots who only care about themselves they shot at the creature as a first encounter. The movie has all of what continue to be my favorite elements in it: geology, fossil evidence from the Devonian period, a postulated link between land and sea creatures, an ichthyologist, and the best monster I ever saw in my life—a piscine amphibious humanoid. The movie is in black-and-white, and the creature is called "Gill-Man."

I don't know why the people who made the movie decided the creature was a man or why they called him Gill-Man. I never saw the creature as a man. Ever. I saw the creature as a finwoman. By the time I saw that movie I was ten years old and already a veteran competitive swimmer.

Mildred Elizabeth Fulvia di Rossi, otherwise known as Milicent or "Mil" Patrick, created the creature, but she was eliminated from the credits. A jealous idiot named Bud Westmore stole her credit and ended her job at Universal Studios. Later in life the wife of Mildred's first husband killed herself because he would not stop seeing Mildred, which contributed to her changing her name to Milicent Patrick. She eventually developed Parkinson's disease and later cancer. She died in 1998. Perhaps her body went back to its breathable blue creature past. Her credits have since been restored. It took a 2019 book by Mallory O'Meara, *The Lady from the Black Lagoon*, to resuscitate her value from the murky depths of Hollywood.

≈

A FAMILY TRINITY sitting silently at a dinner table finishing our food. Or in my head we make a family—mother, father, daughter. My sister, the only ground I have ever known that is not part of the chaos of this place, has left for college. Five years now. Gone forever. Saving her own life. I am the left-behind younger daughter coming of age inside the fragmentation. I have somehow, impossibly, managed to roll up most of my lettuce with sour cream into my napkin. Hidden in my lap. Lettuce with sour cream makes me want to barf. My father loves it because his Eastern European mother made it for him. Vomit. My father's rage has instigated the silent eating. Again. There was a moment when things seemed fine like a family eating dinner, a family in my head or on TV, and then there was a moment when, his fist on the table, the utensils jumped, two cartoon images of a woman and a girl clamping shut, their jaws clicking, their spines clattering.

Mercifully, he stands up and leaves the table. Goes into his home office to sit at his drafting table smoking and drawing. The stool he sits on for years and years spent hunched over an architectural drafting table will eventually give him chronic back pain. But his spine is perfectly formed. He is a handsome man.

My mother clears dishes. I seize the moment: I stand up to throw away my lapful of lettuce and sour cream, but something freezes me between sitting and standing.

In my spine. Something gone wrong. A numb shooting up my vertebrae, across my hips, even making my mouth fill with saliva. I drop my plate and the napkin holding its secrets.

"Mother?" A word children in distress say whether they mean it or not.

My mother comes. Doesn't know what to do.

"Mike?" she calls.

My father comes. His footsteps angry and heavy. I drop to the floor like wilted vegetables. "What are you doing?" he blares.

"My legs," I whisper.

He carries me to my bed. A heaviness consumes me. He asks me if I can feel my legs.

I can feel my legs. I just can't move them right.

I miss swim practice in the morning for the first time in many years.

I miss swim practice that afternoon. And then the whole week.

My life malforms that quickly.

The next day, my mother takes me to the doctor. My legs still feel weird and my back is killing me. He tells me to stand up and bend over to touch my toes. He puts his hand on my spine. He says now slowly come to standing. Halfway to standing he says wait. Then okay. Then stand up. I stand up. We all sit there in the silence of a man's authority for about a minute. Scoliosis, he says. She needs a back brace. He says bend over and touch your toes again, and I do, and he says to my mother, see this S shape? After I return to standing I look at my mother's face, devoured by the memory of her own years in the hospital, squirming inside a full-body cast. The doctor goes on about back braces—truly Frankensteinian contraptions at the time. She doesn't say a word. The doctor tells me to put my hands against the wall and look up. He gives me a giant shot of cortisone straight into my spine. The doctor then gives me six Percocet "to get me through the weekend and back in the pool for training."

Percocet was approved by the FDA in 1976. In 1976 I was thirteen. No one in my family ever speaks about my spine, or any kind of back brace or back treatment, ever again. My spine makes its twisting journey the rest of my life.

I win medal after medal in swimming, biting my cheek underwater against the pain. At night in bed I learn to sleep with the ache like a fist at the base of my spine. My legs never feel the same again. To this day my legs have a faint numbness in them. They are always just this side of floating, my feet never feeling like they are on the ground.

My mother's unstoppable pain and misshapen leg were the most important markers of her place in my life story. A bond is born here: I will carry a malformation in my body. Scoliosis.

My mother drowned her pain in alcohol.

I dove as deeply into the water as possible. Girl underwater who could take it. I made up a creature self in place of weakness. Curved spine of a finwoman.

≈

I WAS BORN CESAREAN. I have thought about that endlessly. What does it mean? Does it mean anything? Does it mean nothing? To be born cesarean means to be born extracted from the motherwaters. Her body sliced open to free you, the creature. I've constructed elaborate theories at different times in my life around my own birth—I have made intense fictions about how I think I missed something important by not fighting my way through water into and out of the birth canal. About how maybe I was lifted too soon from the lifewaters of the mothergut. Or about how I didn't want to leave her body at all, and I was pulled out too soon and thrust into some fucked-up dimension that had nothing to do with me, life on land with humans. They say I resisted extraction. That I turned my stubborn little baby back and butt to them. They say when they rolled me over and pulled me out, my eyes were already wide open. Like I had my stink eye on them from the start.

Yeah, what do you want, *motherfuckers?*

My whole adult life I built stories around the idea that my entrance into the world was malformed. My mother was born with one leg about six inches shorter than the other. Even with several surgeries in her childhood her leg ended up three inches shorter than the other. Misshapen and asymmetrical. Forever.

Malformed: *Abnormally formed, misshapen. Distorted, crooked, contorted, wry, twisted, warped, out of shape, bent, bandy, curved, skewed, asymmetrical, irregular, misproportioned, disfigured, hunchbacked, abnormal, grotesque, monstrous, thrawn* . . . Here is a dictionary sentence putting the idea into motion: *Usually it is the weak, undersized, malformed beasts that are weeded out from the herd.* What kind of fucked-up sentence is that?

I think about form and malformation all the time. You might say I'm a malformation junkie. Especially on the page, especially in language or art, but also in the form of the human body or the bodies of animals or trees or bodies of water. Form is everything to me. The forms that interest me the least—the forms that I find close to useless, the forms that make me want to shoot myself a little bit—are the mainstream, well-received, and popularized traditional forms that the majority of people find pleasing and whole, well-shaped and beautiful. I am passionately obsessed with and devoted to malformations in art and literature and people. Not just structurally, but also at the level of content. I love the monster. The creature. More than I ever love the hero. The antihero is not enough for me. Give me the squirming tentacled blob or grotesque Medusa or oozing alien. I'm so done embracing anything well-formed, perfectly formed, beautiful ever again. What a shitheap of nonsense we've tried to define ourselves with. No wonder women try to kill themselves so often.

I was born cesarean because the doctor told my mother that her babies would be deformed if she dared to let us enter the birth canal of her crazy crooked hips.

Sometimes I just wish someone would put me back into the water and be done with it.

Recovering addicts sometimes get nostalgic about the intense glory of the sensory world coming back to you after a hard kick, its tastes, sights, and sounds—Have you ever *tasted* anything this good in your life? Did you *see* the azure blue of that water? I've never *heard* jazz like that before in my life, man, I think that saxophone just saved my soul. Almost feels like being born again. Almost like the high of a high. Except that it's not. It's just your regular human biological senses coming back to life after the long dull numb of being thickly sedated for long periods of time. The intense glory is funny to those around us. I remember Andy saying, But, Lidia, it's just a cheeseburger. It's just the sound of rain on the back deck. Just the regular stars in the sky.

By the time you experience things as glorious, the crawling-around-on-the-floor-like-a-monster vomiting sessions from the drugs leaving your body is over. The trillions of tiny spiders making your arms and legs jerk involuntarily have mostly subsided. The heavy ache in every bone in your body—like an extended flu from Hades that makes you think you'll likely die, except guiltier, stupider— has been replaced by a kind of measured fatigue or slow motion to your every move. The uncontainable hallucinations retreat back toward your more fluid and oceanic subconscious where they belong. Also where dreams, nightmares, and art live. Your sweat is your sweat again.

Hydrocodone was patented in 1923, while the long-acting formulation was approved for medical use in the United States in 2013. The United States consumes 99 percent of the world supply. In 2016 more than 93 million prescriptions were written. It is made from opium poppy after it has been converted to codeine.

When I was kicking Vicodin after a twelve-year addiction, I had a fever dream at the end of the first month. I was a sea creature with spinelike fins who emerged from the ocean. I ate a man.

≈

MY MOTHER WAS A CRIPPLE. That's the word that was used on her as a child, a teen, a young adult, a woman, a mother, a wife, though that word was never used in our house. The reason that word was never used in our house was that there was a sacred transgression story that my sister and I grew up with. My grandmother—my father's mother—told my father not to marry my mother because she was a cripple. She weaponized and shame-aimed that word. She said, "Well, too bad she's a cripple." When this story was first told in our house we knew it was a shadow story with an evil word. Not to be repeated. We could feel the ugliness of the word. The word was meant to harm our mother.

My mother was born with one leg six inches shorter than the other. I keep coming back to that sentence, that image. Not just here, not just in more than one story, but my whole life. It recurs. But I carry Gertrude Stein's line with me as I repeat myself: "There is no such thing as repetition. Only insistence." She did not have polio, though that would have been accurate historically. She spent years in and out of a children's hospital, in and out of a full-body cast. Think about that for a second. Being a tween in a full-body cast. Alone for the most part in a hospital in Texas. Even after the surgeries to implant a steel plate in her hip where bone should be, one of her legs remained shorter than the other. She had to have her shoes built up. She had to grow up in Port Arthur, Texas.

Mostly she just limped. Dramatically.

Children taunted her mercilessly as a child. Young men shunned her. Young women shamed her. There was no room she ever walked into in her life where everyone didn't notice her limp. And yet her spirit was the counterweight. In high school, when by all rights she should have been ready to kill herself from the shame, she danced harder than anyone at her dances. She danced so hard, crowds parted on the dance floor, like in a movie. She smiled so big the whole room fell for her. Lips red as a Coca-Cola can. Poodle skirt. Who can stop the will of a young woman dancing the night away?

No one, that's who.

I remember how people looked at her in the world. Every day of her life while I was with her growing up. At the grocery store. At the mall. At movie theaters. At parent-teacher conferences at school. With her limp. The way people saw her crept into my identity as I came of age. I saw the weird combination of pity and disgust. Abjection. I did. I see that look alive and well in the world all the time. No matter how pretty we make our words. Or mouths.

Traditional definitions describe a cripple as a person or an animal with a physical disability, particularly one who is unable to walk because of an injury or illness. The word was recorded as early as AD 950, and derives from the Proto-Germanic *krupilaz*. The German and Dutch words *Krüppel* and *kreupel* are cognates. From Proto-Indo-European **grewb-* ("to bend, crouch, crawl"), from Proto-Indo-European **ger-* ("to twist, wind") + **-ilaz*.

Sounds kind of like an animal, doesn't it. Or a creature.

≈

EVERYWHERE, in all times, hunchbacks are either beaten or reviled. Choose your country, your mythologies, your literatures. The hunchback is always a creature. A monster.

Among my favorite hunchbacks in literature are Quasimodo and Richard the Third.

Quasimodo was a fictional character, although there is a theory that there really was a bell tower person with a malformed back who worked at Notre Dame during Victor Hugo's time. Quasimodo finds "love" only through the pain of death.

Richard the Third in Shakespeare has a quite radical disability. In life, he likely had scoliosis. Did you know that today 3D models

of his spine have been created? He had the classic S spine of a scoliosis body, not the monstrous affliction from Shakespeare's famous drama.

≈

MY HUSBAND had crutches for several months after a football injury in high school. It was a big deal. He'd been a defensive lineman
before that. While he was on crutches, some dipshitted Neander-
thal dude, a former fellow jock, messed with him, seizing the vulnerability opportunity. He'd follow my husband around telling him
he was going to beat the shit out of him. After the crutches were
gone and he was healed, my husband ran into the same guy at a
party. Dude proceeded to attempt the taunting again. My husband
gave him one chance by saying, "Really?" Then he beat the crap
out of that guy. Every time he tells that story I wince. I think, that's
a guy thing. A plot that is available to men.

Women and girls and queer people, not so much. Internaliza-
tion of emotions is more common.

But I feel weirdly glad he clocked that peckerhead.

My mother was hospitalized in a full-body cast for years in a
row. The children and then teens around her ground her heart into
dust. And yet she emerged as someone more capable of joy than
almost anyone I've ever met. A joy that could match the depths of
her pain.

We speak of children as if they are pure innocence, but children
also can be on occasion cruel little cretin fuckfaces. Their sense of
right and wrong all balled up inside some untamed rising of desire,
their possible budding young compassion or empathy curled up like
as-yet unfurled ears or not quite finished genitals. Sentences just be-

ginning to form around the seed of power: *What can I get away with? What can I own if I do this? Who will stop me?* Born into the image of their makers. Not yet language. Not yet human. All lunge. Little creatures.

My Texas cousins used to light firecrackers in the mouths of garter snakes and frogs and mice. They'd watch them blow up and then twitch before they died. I was there and all I can say is that I cried like a baby. I'm positive I didn't yet understand why I was crying. But I was for goddamn sure taunted for being the crybaby girl. If I had been a boy, they would have given me a smack or two upside the head. When you are a girl there is a small window of opportunity where young boys will let you hang out with them and participate and then there is the day that they will not, all about your body taking a shape that makes you more like the snakes and frogs and mice.

By the 1970s, the word "cripple" generally came to be regarded as pejorative when used for people with disabilities. Cripple is also a transitive verb, meaning "cause a disability or inability." Think about that. Cripple is a transitive verb. A transitive verb has two characteristics. First, it is an action verb, expressing a doable activity like kick, want, paint, write, eat, clean, etc. Second, it must have a direct object, something or someone who receives the action of the verb. Here, I'll make a sentence: "The way she danced with abandon, as if she freed herself from everything around her, crippled his masculinity for life."

My first memory of my mother's leg happened the first time I saw her swim. I was three. I saw that one of her legs didn't look like the other. Even at three years old I could see that my legs and most people's legs—the legs of my sister and the legs of my father—all looked symmetrical. Her misshapen leg was mesmerizing. I stopped what I had been doing, which was arranging small plastic spoons and one paddle board and more spoons on a picnic table. (Current scholarship says that obsessively making rows and patterns with objects is an early indicator of autism in children, but we didn't know that then. In our house there was no space for disability or non-neuronormative anything. In our house there was the fact of my mother's enduring pain and the fact of my father's violence and the bodies of daughters making their curves and the choice to survive or give up—that's it.) The image of my mother stepping into the lake with one misshapen leg interrupted my obsessive pattern-making at the picnic table. The giant ghost-white pearled scar running up the side of her leg like tracks. Her body slipping into the water, her sidestroke, the off-white of her swimsuit. I remember this perfectly: she was smiling. Even a three-year-old knows what a smile is. It's one of the first things a mother gives an infant, if we're lucky.

My mother's beautiful smile and beautiful swimming came with unending pain threaded through it.

≈

MY LEGS ARE FINE. Well, one of them is shorter than the other, but not in any way you'd notice. I only learned that at a physical when I hit forty-four. Right about the time I was prescribed Vicodin for the pain in my spine caused by an inoperable 28 percent scoliosis curve shooting off to the right and a 25 percent curve shooting inward. Vicodin. A twelve-year ocean. The other thing my mother gave me alongside her smile, her storytelling. Addiction.

≈

MY MOTHER WAS BORN with one leg six inches shorter than the other. The line that won't leave me, or the line I won't leave alone. This may be a reclamation story.

I'm bringing my mother back to body.

I'm bringing my mother back into my body.

I finally see it—though it took me more than half a century to feel it, and it took me this entire act of writing to name it.

In my family, we breed the malformed woman's body. Our bodies bend away from the beautiful objects we were supposedly supposed to be.

My mother's leg.

My spine.

Our bodies don't fit that story.

Our mother-daughter story, like the story of my own daughter, drifts.

In my head there is a movie that runs like water, and in the water the malformed bodies of women leap and dive, surge or drown, thread in between one another like unapologetic teeth-gnashing mermaids and sirens, our creature selves returning to the black lagoon before the moment of our entrance into a culture that would kill us, playful as seals.

Decompositions

Matsutake	*Upright coral*
Lobster mushroom	*Zeller's bolete*
Shaggy parasol	*Dusky bolete*
Coral tooth	*Grisette*
Black picoa	*Morel*
White truffle	*Clouded funnel*
Turkey tail	*False chanterelle*
Blackfoot polypore	*Chanterelle*
Western deer	*Russula*

≈

ANDY IS BECOMING a mushroom hunter.

Where we live now, embedded within Cascade Head and the Salmon River estuary, we are surrounded by mushrooms. Nestled within forests of old-growth Sitkas, western hemlocks, and alders, tucked between ferns so big they look prehistoric, hiding on the soft bounce of the forest floor, mushrooms create their sly networks. He bushwhacks out into the forest hills with our loyal and phenomenal dog Sadie. When we first arrived, they'd bring home a few specimens and lay them out on the counter and he'd explain each varietal to me.

"Did you know that the parasitic fungus that develops on a russula mushroom turns it into a lobster mushroom? Which smells like lobster, and if you cook it just right in butter, begins to taste like bacon?" The names of the mushrooms from his readings get in my body.

They go out, they return.

They bring back what they find. They smell like trees and forest air and the salt rising off the sea that permeates the air here.

One day they returned home with a black mesh bag absolutely bulging. When Andy opened the bag and spilled out the contents, about fifty oyster mushrooms covered the counter. Oyster mushrooms—*Pleurotus ostreatus*—also known as tree mushrooms, grow naturally on old dead alders here. Around the world, they are especially popular in Japanese, Chinese, and Korean cooking. They are beautiful—soft brown oyster-shaped caps with white gills underneath.

Sometimes he finds oyster mushrooms as big as my head.

Andy finds them often; he's learned where to look. Sometimes he has to look up a tree and pull them down with a long stick. Other times they dot a downed limb or trunk just out of sight. You have to train your eyes.

When he first started hunting for mushrooms, he tells me sometimes he'd get lost. Except he actually never says the word "lost." I'm not sure Andy believes in the concept. When I ask him if he ever gets lost, he tells me sometimes he veers off from where he wants to be, and finds himself in a thicket, or a place he did not want to be. So you get lost, I repeat. A woman ready to give him a map. No, I just look at my surroundings, and I know eventually I'll walk into something that will be recognizable to me, like the top of a hill I've been on before, or an elk trail I've seen before. Or a logging road, or I'll just crest a hill and be able to orient by other crests and the ocean coming into view.

His story of himself in the world mesmerizes me. It's so unlike stories of children or women who get lost—or worse—in the woods. Can my love for him have something to do with his fearlessness in the natural world? I have loved women for the same reason.

≈

MY LITHUANIAN GRANDMOTHER once told me about the word "nugrybauti." I didn't see my paternal grandmother much after early childhood; she rests somewhere in my imagination between magical and monstrous, as does my father, like a fairy tale or fable.

In Lithuania, the word nugrybauti* means to lose one's way, to become distracted, to lose the thread of story or sense, but mostly it means to get lost wandering in search of mushrooms. In his excellent essay in part about nugrybauti, the writer Joel Mowdy relates this: "More commonly, though, *nugrybauti* describes when someone has lost the thread of a conversation or veered from the plot of a story—gone on a tangent. To overlay the literal experience with the figurative meaning: while relating a tale, one slides into strange territory by following choice clusters of cognitive associations, then

* For an excellent essay on this word see Joel Mowdy's "Nugrybauti," *Guernica*, April 24, 2019, guernicamag.com/nugrybauti.

becomes struck with panic that the way back is forever lost, only to stumble out somewhere familiar."

When my grandmother told me about the word nugrybauti she was in the kitchen of their house in Ohio peeling a potato. In my memory she was wearing a light blue flowered dress and an off-white apron. Her hair was fluffy and white. Grandma hair. Her breasts were Baltic: heavy and pendulous, taking up most of her chest. But I was four years old so I could be wrong. The kitchen smelled of cabbage and potatoes. I was trying to be small and quiet and good, but I had to pee.

At some point—I've lost the time and place in memory—I got locked in her bathroom. My father is somewhere in this story. Ever after, I had terror around being locked in bathrooms, which I have written about before. Whatever happened, whatever the story is, it wandered, strayed from the original path of a daughter, a father, his mother's house. Another kind of fairy tale.

I've never told Andy how my grandmother gifted the word nugrybauti to me when I was four, because the memory was repressed deeply inside the story of my bathroom trauma, but he's read many stories of mine about what my father did to me.

I didn't remember a single goddamn thing about the word nugrybauti until Andy started to mushroom-hunt out here in our new lives on the coast of Oregon. The word reemerged from the depths of my past. The word came back to me as beauty, not brutality. The word came back to me through water.

THIS IS THE SECOND TIME I've lived in a forest with Andy. When Andy, Miles, and I first moved to Oregon in 2001 we lived in the

Bull Run Wilderness in an octagonal house embedded in an old-growth forest. Miles was a baby. Andy and I worked too hard at our teaching jobs, exhausting ourselves to the bone, then sucked it up to love Miles and each other. I remember the trip we took to Rockaway Beach together as a little family like it was yesterday, but I also remember because Andy made a film that day. And so I have four versions of that day: the event itself, my memory, Andy's film, and my storytelling.

≈

WE CAME TO GET FOOTAGE of me walking into the sea. The film Andy wants to make is based on a short story I wrote called "The Chronology of Water." Gray sky gray sand gray sea, wave crests making rows of angry lace in the ocean. My flesh goosebumps as I shed my clothes at the lip of the water. Black Arena Lycra swimsuit. My red wool coat splays on the sand stark with color against all that gray. The same red coat I wore to the Oregon coast the day I put my daughter Lily's ashes into the sea all those years ago. Different life. Different body. Different love. Memory like epochs. My hair makes wind storm. November, 2003. Rockaway Beach, Oregon.

I walk toward my second world: water.

Andy is behind me on the beach. In his hands, a Super 8 camera. On his back, our son Miles, two years old. *Infant in the water. Infant on land. Love, the distance between them.*

I wonder what it looks like to a baby boy watching his mother walk straight into the raging ocean during a storm. Am I an image in his eyes yet, or something blurry and unresolved? I wonder what it is like to film your wife remembering her whole life, the deathwaters, the lifewaters, walking into the sea. Did he under-stand yet that he had already become a lodestar?

Andy is making the film using footage of me swimming mixed with home movies with Miles and still shots from my past. In this way, past present and future collapse time.

In the ocean, my body is numbing from cold but hyperextend-ing into thought. Memory alive inside a body, coming and going and crisscrossing a life.

It's too cold to be in the water. But I have become a woman who can take it.

When I am thigh-deep in the bone-cold water, when I can tell there are no dangerous sandbanks hiding in front of me from the way the waves are writing their sea story, I dive.

I swim hard into the mad surf. For a moment I think, *you could just keep swimming*, and I also think, *you could drown*, the past and the present becoming fluid.

That dive.

That dive into the ocean at Rockaway Beach had my whole life in it.

From the sea I looked back at Andy and Miles, the only people on the beach and the only people in my life worth coming back for.

I don't remember how long I lasted out there.

I do remember when I swam back to shore, when I emerged shivering and wet as a seal, so cold I could not feel my face, when I ran to Andy and Miles—who looked like a two-bodied water crea-ture at the edge of the world, all of us the only other people on the beach that day—I yelled give me the motherfucking towel! We were laughing our heads off. Even Miles. I'm not even sure he knew what laughing was, but he was the best at it.

You know that crazy kind of laughter. Out-of-control laughter tinged with a release of fear.

And me dressing more quickly than is humanly possible. And my hair heavy with wet. And the swoop of my big red wool coat carrying the traces of my dead daughter Lily's ashes. And Andy taking care with the camera amidst all that sand and water. And Miles's face, his cheeks appling, our laughter flashing through the three of us in a freeze-frame as if we could be a single organism, washed through, after fire and pain and sadness, with . . . joy? Inside me, I mean. Inside my body.

≈

IT IS DIFFICULT for me to write about joy. Joy washes over you differently than pain or trauma or rage . . . you don't drown in joy. Joy brings you back to a kind of childhood giddiness or even before that, maybe before language. Like when babies fart or poop their pants and smile and laugh. Pure release. Or like the flush of heroin. Or like the middle of an orgasm where you sort of wish you could die there. Or like a dog rolling around on its back. Or like Miles at my nipple, drinking in motherloving life. Joy flushes through your body, doesn't it? Joy doesn't make sense against the drooling desperation of pain, grief, loss. Joy is even more nonsensical and ineffable than beauty or pain. Joy resists narration.

To experience joy, it seems that you have to be open to all the other possibilities. Being that open hurts. Maybe it doesn't hurt everyone to be open like that . . . but I wonder. I think for some of us it's like that. I think some of us wonder endlessly if the risk is worth it. But joy and pain are only opposites if you let them stay fixed in some idiotic binary. Most of the little shocks in life that mean anything to me amidst the gray hum of the dull daily stuff of life are a murmuration of both joy and sorrow.

≈

AFTER ANDY CAPTURED ME in a towel and bundled me into the car, he walked around to the back of the car to put his camera equipment away. He still had Miles on his back, and accidentally biffed Miles's head when he lifted the rear door open. Not terribly, just barely. Miles cried in heaves for about three minutes.

Tucked safely back into his car seat, Miles looked at me, I looked at him, and we started laugh-crying, suspended between joy and pain. Andy drove us to a coastal roadside diner for hot coffee and cherry pie. Perched in his high chair, Miles smeared little handfuls of cherry pie on his mouth and face. Andy ate apple pie. In the diner I finally stopped shivering. The other people in the diner looked a little like tree bark and barnacles to me—older coastal folk who were likely regulars. I am relatively certain that it was the best cherry pie I ever put in my mouth for the rest of my life. I don't know if it was the taste or the husband and son of it, a story I never believed I would inhabit.

I remember when there was a time before Miles.

≈

BEFORE MILES EXISTED, we dreamed him. We conjured him as lovers early on in our relationship on a day we spent at Lake Tahoe. Lake Tahoe was a place Andy had visited many times. Andy had been there a lot because he grew up in Reno, and I had visited many times on what passed for family vacations with my parents. My parents gambled; I tried not to pass out in the hot summer sun. The fact that we may have both been there once or twice at the same time fascinates me. We have more than one segment of our lives before we met where we crossed paths like stars, ignorant of each other's existences, until we collided; Lake Tahoe and Eugene, Oregon, are both examples.

The Tahoe lake water was everything to me when I was a child. My own early erotic agency was born in that lake during the summers when I was ten, eleven, and twelve. The water was too cold for my mother. Too cold for my father, too—in addition to the fact that he could not swim. My sister was long gone by then. So entering that water as a kid was a form of freestyle story space. Once when I emerged shivering from the water my mother put a towel around me; the towel was covered with ladybugs.

When Andy took me to the shores of Lake Tahoe later in life it wasn't quite summer and it most definitely was not warm enough to swim in the ice water. But I entered the water anyway. Cold water gives me mind shock in the good way. It blasts the past and pain out of my body.

The image that came to me in the ice water was of a beautiful, larger-than-life ladybug. Not a cartoon ladybug, more like an eighteenth-century detailed illustration. Intricate and careful. When I emerged, I put on a wool hat and my black leather biker jacket and green cargo pants. Quickly. But none of that mattered when Andy and I fell to the sand near a giant piece of driftwood and fuck-wrestled each other so hard I bruised my tailbone. When we kissed each other the devouring must have had everything neither of us got as kids in it. I can tell our kid selves were feeling liberated. I know that feeling deeply. When we fucked it must have had the lives we wish we'd had in every heave and rend. And when we orgasmed, the people in the cars who plainly saw us from the road must have chuckled at least a little, remembering bliss like retinal flashes. But, too, when we orgasmed and when I shuddered, I felt death leaving. Or a specific version of death, one that nearly consumed me.

When I looked up at the log we fucked near, it was covered with *hundreds* of ladybugs. Yes, really. I took a photo.

Back inside the image and the memory and my past at Rockaway Beach, with Miles as a baby boy in Andy's backpack, Andy holding a film camera, the wind rose and fell in waves. We'd chosen the day because on a stormy day we suspected very few other people would be peopling the beach, and we were right. I became a film. I've watched the video Andy edited into a short film many times.

In place of home movies, we have Andy's art. We have my stories.

≈

IN MY PRESENT TENSE, as I reanimate and rearrange these memories, time contracts and expands like an accordion. Miles just finished college, so we also have Miles's art. The devotion and seriousness with which the three of us make art shows me something about us that is a little bittersweet or even melancholy but also absolutely beautiful. We are all three driven to make art partly because we can't help it and partly because we are all three a little misfitted in the regular world. For me it is coming from the house of father, abused and anger-knotted with the loss and the grief of losing my daughter the day she was born. For Andy it is something about the loss and grief of his father dying so young at thirty-three when Andy was three, the neglect he felt from that space called mother ever after, the hole where love should be, his own heart beating him up—*what is a man, what is a man, what is a man.* He has to invent himself daily.

Miles is just starting his life now, so I can't speak for him. Maybe Miles is driven to make art differently than we are. I do know it is not my story to tell.

I have a fear in me. Something I hope isn't true. It is that the holes inside his parents that drove them into each other's arms as well as into making art are also in his body somehow. Like he carries a trace of our sadness and pain even as he will become a completely different person.

When Miles was fifteen he asked me if it was still possible to make important art if you came from a loving and stable homelife. It was a real question. My answer was probably stupid.

Miles was born up and through a crucible. Holes in our hearts, rage in our ribs, lost jobs, the chaos of desire gone berserk, a mother who spawned a head-on collision, broken laws, broken lives, cars breaking down, double divorces, no future mapped out, not enough food, not enough faith, not enough money—who the hell did we think we were to make a family?

But I have at least some evidence that difficulty doesn't travel so easily as that. I used to be desperately afraid that my father was in me. My father, the person who abused his daughters and his wife. It turns out my father isn't in me like that. It's the world that carries violence against women and children. I'm the daughter who bit through the story thread and rewove it.

The trace I carry from my father, it turns out, is art. And maybe athleticism, though I'm no longer an athlete. But that kind of shoulder to bicep and hip strength, the musculature that comes from being a swimmer, still present even as I sag and bloat with age. I definitely dive headfirst into pretty much everything, for better or worse. I definitely shoulder my way through life, even when I am terrified.

I definitely take it.

The trace Miles carries from us—I hope it is artmaking. I hope it is love. If I knew anything about hope, I'd hope that. Miles has the most tender touch in his hands of anyone I've ever met. If he does carry a trace of sadness, I hope he learns that sorrow is a form of transmography, not an endwall.

Sometimes I worry that men have fallen from a story we gave them that cannot hold any longer. But haven't we all? The old stories have collapsed in on themselves. Don't we need to invent new stories capable of carrying us?

≈

I REMEMBER on the way back home from the beach that day, I thought about how all we had in the house that night to eat was some rice and day-old chicken and a half bottle of wine. I thought about how if the wind kicked up too much we'd lose power again, but we could pile up all the sleeping bags and burrow into them and I was pretty sure all the flashlights had new batteries. I thought about how hard Andy and I were working at our multiple jobs just to keep our shit mildly together, lobbing Miles back and forth like a football in an effort to keep him out of daycare, or maybe in an effort to always have him against one of our bodies. Our shit cars we were praying didn't break down again again again. Our debt rising in waves at our backs because our "income" was too puny. How dare we make a life out there like that in the woods, up against impossibility? A mother, a father, a son vibrating the edges of those very words, since none of us knew how to inhabit them.

Mostly on that car ride home I pictured what Andy's camera was carrying inside. An act of pure and unapologetic imagination. A baby boy on his father's back who can laugh big as the sea. A dead baby girl whose ashes went to the ocean, a woman's body capable of carrying death and life and living to tell about it stepping into the sea. A man behind a camera trying to capture the images and give them a form, in spite of the whole world making all of us feel not good enough or weird or wrong or failing or falling or just making us feel like nothing.

The world was wrong.

≈

I REMEMBER THE DAY I understood that Miles was a human portal. We were at Père Lachaise Cemetery.

I first visited Père Lachaise Cemetery in Paris with my first husband when I was nineteen. Something about the vast necropolis drew me in so deeply at the time that I made my first husband take me there every single day for seven days. I did not know why and don't to this day. Not even the Louvre got into my body as deeply as Père Lachaise. As a painter, he wanted to be in Paris for art reasons. I may have wanted to be in France for death reasons. I was drinking too much and acting out at that age. "Animalistic" is the word that comes to mind. Biting and scratching and taking stupid risks, especially at night. Breaking into homes. Jumping off bridges. Stealing. Reaching for the next drug to see what it would do, where it would take me.

I had not yet become pregnant. I had not yet lost a child—which is a curious phrase, because it sounds like I misplaced an infant, like in some Lithuanian fairy tales I know. The seed of our lost child had not yet been planted, but would be soon. I did not have favorite dead people yet, I had not read enough books. You might say I was latent with meaning as a body. All my drives were firing, none of them contained by a useful shape yet. But we both loved Chopin, so we brought a baguette and a tomato and ate them next to dead Chopin.

The cemetery is in the 20th arrondissement in Paris, on the Boulevard de Ménilmontant. Père Lachaise first opened in 1804. Napoléon, the emperor, decreed that every citizen had the right to be buried there regardless of race or religion. It continues to blow my mind that in 1804, Père Lachaise had thirteen graves. I mean if you have seen it, or if you ever enter its labyrinthian acreage, the explosion of dead bodies shivers the soul. In 1817, the supposed remains of Abelard and Héloïse (Pierre Abélard and Héloïse d'Argenteuil), those two lovers who orbited one another like longing stars, scripted letter after letter trying to stitch their way back to each other, were moved to the cemetery. And so a French love ritual emerged. Lovers or the lovelorn leave their letters at the crypt. The cemetery has been expanded at least five times that I know of, possibly more.

There is a waiting list to be buried there today; 3.5 million visitors grace or trample its grounds every year.

The first time with my first husband, I took a nap next to Chopin. I put my body down in the dirt and small stones between plots. The gravestones and trees felt comforting to me in a way that people do not. The silence between the sound of wind in the trees had a kind of lullaby quality. I think my first husband was petting my hair, which will drop me faster than most gestures. I dreamed of a white Lily flower that could talk. The flower said you can make any story you want from the shapes you see in the night sky. We were in Paris for seven days. We were able to go to Paris because he got an art scholarship. I just didn't eat for a few weeks (well, my staple diet of Pop-Tarts and vodka) and squirreled away some student loan and work-study dollars. We stayed in possibly the worst apartment in Paris—the toilet was overflowing with shit, the bed felt made from straw, there was little heat and no hot water in what passed for a shower—but the window opened up to a view of Notre Dame in the 4th arrondissement of Paris, so we were essentially seeded in the Left Bank enough to feel happy. My three favorite moments from the trip: standing in front of the statue of Joan of Arc inside Notre Dame; wandering around the Shakespeare and Company bookstore and feeling each other up (to his dismay) on the top floor; and Père Lachaise, my nap with Chopin, the Lily dream.

≈

THE SECOND TIME I visited Père Lachaise I was with Devin. By then I had lost a child (maybe also I was beginning to search for her). By then I definitely had favorite dead people, because I was reading books voraciously. Simone de Beauvoir and Sartre. Gertrude Stein, Marcel Proust, Richard Wright, Alice B. Toklas, Eugène Delacroix, Max Ernst, Amedeo Modigliani, Sarah Bernhardt, Colette, Oscar Wilde, Edith Piaf. And by then I absolutely knew who Héloïse was; she had become very important to me. Her life as a philosopher, scholar, and writer fascinated me. That she was a kind of philosopher of love mesmerized me. Her love affair with Abelard tickled me. That her letters became foundational in Western literature made me giddy. The epistolary novel got into my body. Bildungsroman got into my body. And I'm not the only one—her work drew the attention of Chaucer, Thomas Aquinas, Voltaire, Rousseau, and Simone Weil. (I once made a side trip to Bybrook Cemetery, Ashford, United Kingdom, just to have a small whisper-chat at the grave of Simone Weil. I wanted to thank her.)

I made Devin find every single one of those graves. At some of them, I could hear voices—not actual sentences, but something like murmurs, which then made me think of the murmuration of birds, but I transposed that meaning onto bodies. By then, death lived in my body, and I had questions.

Because Devin was Devin, we made a beeline for Jim Morrison, patron saint of beautiful drunk and doomed artists, with a bottle of wine, a baguette, and a hunk of cheese.

Of course we saw others there who made that same pilgrimage. The headstone sculpted by Croatian artist Mladen Mikulin still lived at the grave, adorned with lipstick and graffiti. The bust was stolen in 1988, I believe; we were there in 1986. We drank our bottle of wine near others, respectfully. Devin cried a little. I was never into the Doors much, but I admired the music enough to pay my respects, I suppose. Or I just wanted Devin to be happy.

The weight of my dumb, stubborn heart.

By the time Oliver Stone's film *The Doors* came out, I was willing to ride the death train into oblivion with Devin. When the music is over, turn out the light.

The third time I was at Père Lachaise was the most meaningful experience to me by far. With Andy and Miles. I carry the trace of the previous visits with me, but they are like floating sediments. There was no bottle of wine or vodka this time. There was no expat picnic. We did swing by Morrison's grave, but only briefly, so Miles could at least witness the weird.

I remember the vast forest of over five thousand trees—maple, ash, ginkgo biloba, maidenhair, chestnut, a gutta-percha tree—and the sound of wind speaking through leaves, and the small sounds of birds, over four hundred species—common wood pigeons, magpies, tits, jays, short-toed treecreepers, starlings, crows.

The light rain that fell, like the touch of dreams falling from the sky that day, a purple umbrella I bought at a souvenir shop, Andy ahead of us on the cobblestone path near the top of the cemetery, and Miles.

Miles is walking the distance between us. His back is to me. He is eleven. His shoulders swivel when he walks—almost but not yet the way a grown man's do. His hands are jammed in the pockets of a black wool coat. His hair, a color between brown and blond, is shoulder-length. I stare at his back, his slightly awkward gait, the walk of a not-yet teen. A shock wave runs up my body from my vagina to my clavicle. Someday soon he is going to be walking away from us into his own life. Or, the walk away from us has already begun, just now. My son is a portal. He is stepping through into self.

In some ways I just want to lie down and die, sleep with the sleepers.

In place of death, however, I feel joy. Joy that I was at Père Lachaise when that shock wave hit. I'm comforted in the company of death—not morbid or violent death, just regular death—dead birds, felled in flight but just as beautiful resting on the ground, stilled; cemeteries; dead trees, rotting and yet making mushrooms or giving their bodies over as nursery trees. I feel joy that Miles has been to France—or that traveling as a child got into his body. He may need that in his heart pocket later in life. I do cry, but neither Andy nor Miles sees me, because of the trees like sentries all around us, because of the light rain, because I can shield my sorrow with my purple umbrella. Eventually I catch up to Andy, who has taken a picture of the whole thing, a photo I will stare and stare at later. When I reach Andy, I find that he too is crying, but we manage to cover our emotions enough to listen to a boy being a boy in this strange place. Miles loves the place. His favorite grave? Oscar Wilde's.

What I learned in that last Père Lachaise trip with Andy and Miles taught me how to later ask Andy to take me to the Hobbit Trail and Heceta Head Lighthouse—just recently, in 2022. Yes, that is the place where I opened my hand and let loose my daughter Lily's ashes in the Oregon ocean water over forty years ago, a scene re-created at Rockaway Beach in Andy's film. Do not come at me, or anyone, on the topic of how long we hold on to grief. Past, present, and future again surfaced in my body.

How it happened: In 2022, my body made a scene. My breasts became as big as sacks of potatoes, a kind of Baltic ballooning. I treaded water in the depths of menopausal hell, not sleeping at night, hot-flashing like a human torch, feeling faint or dizzy anytime I bent over or got out of bed, about to have to go on high blood pressure medicine, about to have my breast lump biopsied, carrying forty extra pounds of god knows what. I think now that my body was trying to show me that I was carrying too much. Not just weight. But sorrow. Guilt. Rage. Fear. Love. Death.

We were in the process of moving from Milwaukie, Oregon, out to a forest next to the ocean near Lincoln City. We'd lived in our Milwaukie house for twenty years; we'd raised Miles and each other there; we'd loved and let go of four animals there; Andy had planted and tended the world's greatest vegetable garden; we'd also planted trees: cherry blossom, ginkgo biloba, quivering aspen, madrone, four Japanese maples, vine maples that caught the sunlight through the cedars and showered us with green shimmering light in the summer. Clematis and Boston ivy climbed the walls and railings, enormous dark purple-black irises emerged in summer, a whole field of hyacinths made a carpet of purple in front of the house in the spring. A line of rosebushes in reds, yellows, corals, pinks, whites. In February, your heart would leap at the first camellia flower; our camellia trees were likely over fifty years old, maybe older. The tree in the front of the house was a one-hundred-year-old redwood. Lemon and lime trees filled the night air with aphrodisia-cal blossoms. We spent many summer evenings at a thirty-year-old farmers' table sharing good food and the pleasure of good company with friends.

We were then well prepared to move into an actual forest next to the sea, having cultivated our garden in the city in every way a person could. We entered the natural world again with a bit more wisdom and love and softness in us, on the one hand, and me about to fly apart one scar at a time on the other.

Part of the process of leaving our lives to move to the coast involved driving our son to Eugene for college, and on one of those return trips with Andy, I asked that we take the coast road to Florence instead of the freeway up to Salem where we'd usually cut over to our newest nest, our coast range house where we would begin again to make a home. I'd taken the coast road from Eugene to

Florence many times during the years I lived in Eugene. First with my first husband. Then with Devin. Once with Kesey; several times with women I was involved with. I'd never taken that drive or traveled to Lily's death resting place with Andy.

Sometimes the moment you know you have to make a return comes out of nowhere; you just know you have to return with your whole body, just like when you know you can't do something. I've stopped questioning that moment.

Or sometimes the moment just lives in you until you are ready, or, it lives all around all of us, and we have to choose when to reach or leap. All those moments swimming in us and around us like molecules. Sediments of memory. Seeds. Waves and particles in their eternal dance.

The Hobbit Trail hike is about a mile long in western Oregon although it winds up a few hills, so it can feel longer. The trail threads through a deep Sitka spruce tree forest filled with moss in a hundred different colors of green, ferns as big as a person, little coves that remind you of yes, hobbits. You can also extend the hike by continuing on to Heceta Head Lighthouse, which ends up being a 5.2-mile hike round-trip.

Even though I am a terrible hiker and I was also in possibly the worst health of my life at the time, I asked Andy to go on the Hobbit Trail hike with me. He knew what was at Heceta Head, so it took him less than me finishing my sentence to say yes.

The smell of a Sitka spruce old-growth forest would draw anyone in. Hansel and Gretel, Snow White, all the goddesses in the Lithuanian pantheon—Ausrine, Dalia, Gabija, Laima, Saule, Vakarine, Zemyna, the seven sister goddesses who made garments from humans' lives: Verpiančioji, the spinner of life, Metančioji, shaper of life, Audėja, the weaver, Gadintoja, the one who broke the thread, Sergėtoja, who made the tear, Nukirpėja, cloth cutter, and Išskalbėja, the washer* . . . these female folktale figures were with me.

Andy guided me slowly, patiently, lovingly, through the Hobbit Trail all the way back to Heceta Head Lighthouse, almost like moving through memories or chapters of a life.

When I fell behind, he waited for me.

When I sat down on a log or just in the mud from fatigue, overwhelmed by memories or feelings, he came to get me.

When I slipped in the mud and fell on my ass, he helped me up. He held my hand.

When I stopped too often to take photos, or to study a red-capped mushroom with white spots—*Amanita muscaria*, or fly agaric, I'd learn from him later, a deadly poisonous mushroom—he'd just lean on a tree, or travel a little ahead to see what was next for us. But he never—not once in our over twenty-five years together—left me or let me put something inedible or nonnutritive in my mouth.

The trees, since they are Sitka spruce, have those wild octopus arms that stretch out making you think they might actually move or touch you. Magical tunnels form from tree branches, dark patches which touch the foreboding magic of fairy tales that give way to dappled light and glimpses of ocean. If you skip Heceta Head Lighthouse, the half-mile hike drops you deliciously down into the beach at Carl G. Washburne Memorial State Park, what used to be

---

* See Gintaras Beresnevičius's "Lithuanian Religion and Mythology," translated by Lora Tamošiūnienė, archived April 2, 2007, at the Wayback Machine, web.archive.org/web /20070402233953/http://viduramziu.lietuvos.net/socium/pagonybe.htm.

a kind of secluded beach until someone decided to rename the trail the Hobbit Trail.

The Heceta Head Lighthouse beacon shines for twenty miles into the sea. The lighthouse was first illuminated in 1894 and sits two hundred feet above sea level atop a cliff. The historic Cape Creek Bridge arches over the place where a creek and the ocean meet. If you are at the lip of the ocean and the arm of the creek, the bridge feels like it has your back. If you do not stop at the bridge and you keep driving, you will find the cities of Florence and Waldport, where some of my Kesey experiences happened.

Cape Creek flows along the south side, merging fresh water with the sea. That is the creek that forty years ago Philip, my first husband, and I tried to throw Lily's little pink box of ashes into, thinking it would gently flow into the ocean, before I realized I would have to bring her closer to my body by opening the little pink box and holding her ashes in my hand while I waded out into the sea.

I suspect the reason I am so devoted to women around forty years old has something to do with mothers and daughters.

At the beach, there are tidepools filled with neon green and pink anemones and purply black urchins, orange and violet starfish textured and clinging to rocks or sitting serenely in sand beds, translucent jellyfish, rock faces dotted with barnacles bigger than your knuckles and black and blue mussels jutting up like bruised thumbs. Driftwood and crab carcasses, scallop and clam shells and sand dollars make constellations in the sand. Dogs and children go apeshit with glee. You could easily see a whale spout. You nearly always see a harbor seal.

But what most pulls my body to Oregon ocean beaches—besides

the water of course—is that the dead things and the living things are churned up together in the waves, left resting on the beach, or carried back out into a large story of existence, just as they are in my body and my storytelling.

When we made it up the last incline before the lighthouse—a torture to me—we paused to absorb the view of the ocean from the high bluff of the forest. There is literally nothing like it anywhere. Then we made the equally steep plummet down to the lighthouse.

I know exactly why I needed to go "to the lighthouse" first: "She felt . . . how life, from being made up of little separate incidents which one lived one by one, became curled and whole like a wave which bore one up with it and threw one down with it, there, with a dash on the beach"—it's a line from Woolf's novel and a line in her nonfiction; a line I have quoted in my own novels and nonfiction.

After I stood at the Heceta Head Lighthouse, after I looked up at the height of her, after I took in the pulse of the light, after I thought about how much Miles loves the dark and gorgeous film *The Lighthouse* with Willem Dafoe and Robert Pattinson in which that terrifyingly erotic selkie thing washes up on the beach. The thought of the film making me smile while tears also run down my appled-up cheeks, after the sea spray has frizzled my hair, we make our way down to the beach, the deathbed of my daughter.

My body at the water's edge.

This time I reach into my pocket and let go of three rocks I have kept for years. Three stones with three secrets for her to discover, or maybe for a seal to discover. I thought about the red cap of the deadly mushroom that had drawn my attention. I thought about the red coat I wore the first time I waded into the sea with her ashes, how I still have it and still wear it when I want to feel held by something out of time.

I walked back to Andy on the shore. I didn't say anything all the way home, although I'm not sure that's accurate because what lived between us inside the silence of the drive was my whole life.

≈

ANDY AND I HAVE LIVED in the Sitka and alder forest next to the ocean on the Oregon coast for a while now. Andy has re-formed a relationship with mushrooms, wilderness, and cello. I have witnessed more birdsong here than I have in my entire life. On a single afternoon I can hear the chirp of hummingbirds, the songs of Steller's jays, Wilson's warblers, Swainson's thrush, Pacific wren, yellow-breasted chat, song sparrow, hermit warbler, chestnut-backed chickadee, and high up in a Sitka, the chatter of eagles, and, of course, the caw of the American crow. When I stand at the lip of the ocean, I feel like I am part of everything we came from, instead of one puny human against the world. When Andy and Sadie bring home oyster mushrooms we often take a picture of them to send to Miles, since he has joined the foraging and nugrybauti on occasion. Then Andy carefully cleans each mushroom with a little brush. He slices the mushrooms on a large wooden cutting board while I peel and mince garlic and chop up parsley. Andy cooks the oyster mushrooms in butter, garlic, and sometimes white wine. He might put them on a mound of angel-hair pasta, or we might just eat them as a luxurious side.

Andy has taken up cello again, which he excelled at as a boy. He's made an epic return. It feels as if we have freed ourselves from origin stories that nearly killed us, in the process retrieving what was lost and bringing it back like a beautiful gift you never received until the day you gave it to yourself.

When Andy plays cello in the afternoon, between three o'clock and time to make dinner, the whole house swells. The living room comes to life with Bach, the ceilings lift as if they are made of sky, the walls breathe. You can feel cello music in your spine, your hips, your shoulders, your whole body opening up and dropping low to the ground. Maybe that is love. Or grace. I don't know. I only know I surrender to his music by listening, and through listening my body surrenders and I feel as close to being a tree as I'm able.

We may carry traces of our pasts with us, but every single day we let pieces of what hurt us go, into ground, into mushrooms, into music and storytelling and art, into strangers within reach, into water, into the great Sitkas and Alders all around us, of which, mercifully, we are a part.

≈

Dorothy, my mother: *Why don't you write any happy stories, Belle?*

Me: *Where are the happy stories?*

Dorothy: *Happy stories live inside of us.*

Me: *Maybe mine drowned.*

Dorothy: *Swim for it, Belle.*

≈

Ever After

*O*nce there was a girl who could not stop diving into water. She leapt off piers at the beach she leapt into lakes in the forest she leapt into rivers that smelled of fish and rock moss. If it rained, she ran out into the rain. If her mother wondered where she was, she always checked the bathtub first. Twice during a hurricane she lodged herself too high for retrieval between branches of trees and heaves of wind and rain. Another time a neighbor brought her back from the koi pond in their garden. Once her mother even found her at the neighbors' house just standing at their fish tank with her arms and hands submerged, staring at tetras and goldfish and a little plastic man in an old-fashioned diving suit.

Maybe the girl could not stop diving into water because her house was on fire.

Or maybe she just wasn't meant for land, maybe she simply preferred the amniotic and was looking for a way back.

Or maybe it was the leap.

At any rate, it seemed she would do anything to be in water.

When she was young, she lived her life on a swim team, and everyone thought well surely that will help.

Later, she lived close enough to rivers to swim and share secrets within their swells and eddies, she lived close enough to the sea to answer every whisper. For a while, this seemed like a relationship she could grow by.

But always the fist and thrust of father would find her—a thousand different fathers with a thousand different faces and fists. There was no water that could carry her far enough away.

When she got older, she swam away from men and dove into a bottle of vodka; strange motherwaters in order to transform the story.

She became a girl who lived inside a bottle in the ocean alongside a message she couldn't read. The message was rolled up on a piece of paper as big as she was. She knew the message was there, but anesthetized by vodka and comforted by floating in the safety of fluid inside a vessel, she felt little compulsion to open the message and read it. She felt lulled. Unseen. Secreted.

Until the day the message cut her; that is, the paper that carried the message rubbed her the wrong way during a storm and left a mark, a red line at her neck like a second smile, where her voice lived.

The girl put one hand at her throat to stop the red blood. With her other hand she opened the big-as-a-body message.

The message read: Sometimes daughters must leave the stories laid out for them in order to find solace. Love, Mother.

The girl used some of the paper to stanch the wound at her throat. A voice grew in that place. With the rest of the paper, she fed herself to gain strength. Eating the paper healed her voice, a voice not sweet, but textured.

Leaving the vodka bottle felt like abandoning her mother, but she did it anyway. She dove into the ocean.

Ocean animals understood her storytelling with ease ever after.

≈

I STAND at the lip of the ocean. The horizon in my gaze that place where sky kisses sea. It is always this way; my girl emerges, the one that died, in the moment a seal's head surfaces.

We stare at each other.

The girl is a seal.

Or the seal is a girl.

Or the space between the word girl and the word seal is as wide as an ocean, in motion, the wave and the dive and the surge and the fall. What is language in the face of an ocean?

The girl is a seal.

Or the seal is a girl.

The myths rise from depths before we were born. They funnel and swell and reach for sky, for form. Up from the bottom of everything they ache for the kiss of sky. And there at the bottom, did the girl begin as girl? Or was that her ending? As her body underwent the adaptations, the evolutions, her fingers becoming webbed, her torso and hips blending into a great muscle of curve and bellied swell, her feet flippering, did the word girl change too?

Alone as an old woman I take my dog Sadie to the sea. We see a seal in the water. Sadie and the seal make eye contact, they stare at each other. Sadie wades out into the sea with her ball, chest high, and leaves it.

The girl is a seal.

Or the seal is a girl.

I shed my clothes and wade into the water to get the ball. Is that why I wade into the water? Sadie keeps watch. The seal keeps watch. Mammals in a moment, species between us.

The girl is a seal.

Or the seal is a girl.

Or her place in the story somewhere shifted or slipped from amphibian to mammal. Who stepped or slid onto the shore? Girl or seal? Who slipped from my body? Girl or seal? Who am I when I enter water?

Oh seal who was a girl or girl who was a seal or word or motion or language itself I give in. I give over. How do you tell the story of a story that lives in a body in waves without end? In oceans, tides, de-creations and re-creations?

The girl is a seal.

Or the seal is a girl.

I have cried oceans of tears for four decades, as if the sea could not live without my weeping.

I put my clothes back on. I'm cold! I'm alive. Sadie watches me with concern.

The seal is the girl and the girl is the twirl of the world. The sea is the seal and the curl of a wave is the word for girl and the furl of the girl in the curl of the wave is a pearl forming from the agitation inside an oyster in the paws of a playful seal. The girl of a wave that curls in the sea makes a seal laugh a bark a dog on the shore wags its tail.

Now I can see it.

She plays.

Evaporation

M aybe you have been waiting for more of the story, since I wrote about Devin in the beginning, in the middle, and at the end. Maybe not. No one knows where stories will go in a body. No one can say how a story will travel, fragment, live, die, or rearrange in their own body, or in any reader's.

Sometimes the story goes where it wants to, and we try to grab at it, cling to it for all we're worth. Sometimes we turn away from it or cast it away from us because the story is nothing about us, right? Or maybe because we can't handle the idea that the story names some part of us we'd rather not admit exists. Sometimes we hold on to a story too long, and the weight of it nearly crushes us. What if the story changes every time we touch it? How difficult it is to let a story go.

I've carried a shapeshifting story of Devin in my body for thirty years. In some versions he's the hero, in others the villain, or I am. More and more I see that there was no hero, no villain, no plot, no climax, no resolution. Those are narrative markers we place upon life when we are afraid of life's chaotic grind and hum. Storytelling patterns may give us the chance at catharsis, release, an artful possibility when pain seems too much to carry, but sometimes we have to double back, dig up a story underneath the one we've carried, rearrange an old one, let some stories fall away.

Devin has gone to stardust, which is my actual belief, that we return to the cosmos from which all matter and energy are created and de-created endlessly. His body is no longer with me.

But where do love stories go when they die?

I've told almost none of the deepest story of our time together, just pieces here and there. I almost always leave off before I render the heart of the matter. Maybe because I'm afraid of putting us asunder forever.

All I have of Devin are pieces of a story.

The autopsy report paints a picture of his body. Multiple abrasions covering his face and upper chest. His right clavicle fractured. Each of his knees marked by a 1.5-inch circular abrasion. His right upper arm twisted wrongly over his head. Multiple ribs fractured. Blood leaking from his right ear. His skull fractured, one eye distended, his brain torn. Fractured vertebrae. Multiple contusions and tears to his lungs, liver, and heart.

The report describes the tattoos I knew so well. Carpe Diem. Don't Try. The Chinese symbol for longevity.

The images and descriptions in the report took me years to look at, after that day Andy presented them to me in the manila envelope. Almost ten years.

Though the first page describes a fall, later pages suggest a leap.

Together with other pieces of his story, I make arrangements and rearrangements in my head trying to understand the past. I use

12

AUTOPSY REPORT

I performed an autopsy on the body of ➡

No. 2015-00089

CROWE, DEVIN E.

at _____ the DEPARTMENT OF CORONER

Los Angeles, California _____ on ___ JANUARY 07, 2015 @ 0949 hours ___
 (Date) (Time)

From the anatomic findings and pertinent history I ascribe the death to:

(A)   MULTIPLE TRAUMATIC INJURIES
DUE TO OR AS A CONSEQUENCE OF

(B)
DUE TO OR AS A CONSEQUENCE OF

(C)
DUE TO OR AS A CONSEQUENCE OF

(D)
OTHER CONDITIONS CONTRIBUTING BUT NOT RELATED TO THE IMMEDIATE CAUSE OF DEATH:
     ACUTE ALCOHOL INTOXICATION

Anatomical Summary:

1. 52-year-old Caucasian male, reportedly found within a pit
   adjacent to a crane that he apparently fell from while
   climbing the tower.

2. Multiple external and internal traumatic injuries.

3. See toxicology report: elevated levels of alcohol.

20

52 y/o Caucasian male
72" - 195#

0949
8
Clear plastic
bag

2015-00089
CROWE, DEVIN EUGENE

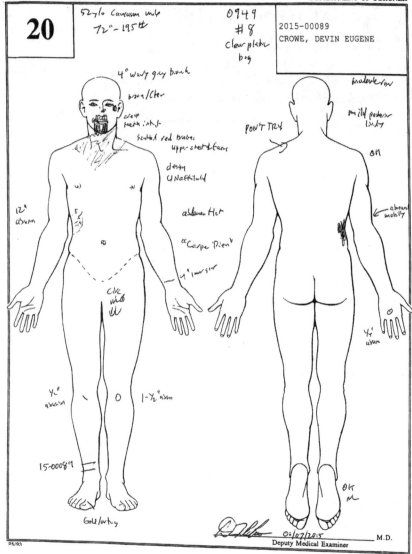

4" wavy gray beard

brown/blue

crude teeth intact

scattered red bruises
upper chest & face

dense
U Natt'y build

abdomen flat

"Carpe Diem"

4" laceration

circumcised

12" abrasion

3/4" abrasion

1-1/2" abrasion

3/4" abrasion

15-00089

Gold/watch

moderate rigor

mild posterior
lividity

OH

abnormal
mobility

3/4" abrasion

OK
M

PON'T TRY

06/07/2015   _____ M.D.
Deputy Medical Examiner

objects. Artifacts: photos, drawings, paintings, writing. The black book of his sketches and writing, written partly when he was in jail. Our dog Zozo's pulled teeth. His silver claddagh ring. All so that I may withstand the fact of his life, the fact of his death.

And a long black braid of Devin's hair from the first time he cut it during our years together. The hair still smells like him.

There are three images that rise when I think of loving Devin. They are like photos untaken that live in my body, as if my body were some kind of reliquary.

The first image is from the trip to Greece, the trip where I cracked the egg and said that terrible line about love breaking. An ending in the beginning. But the image is not the egg. The image is of him drinking retsina in a tiny bar at the edge of a cliff overlooking the Aegean. We'd been swimming in the sea earlier. His face rests on his palm. His dark wet hair makes S shapes down his back. He smells of salt—I can taste him. He wears a T-shirt the color of coral. He looks directly into my faint blue eyes, his eyes as dark as black holes. He doesn't say anything or do anything. He just looks like a Greek statue to me, impenetrable but epic in beauty. This man's life story should have been mythic, it seems to me, but the life got squeezed out of him like some dumb tube of toothpaste. He thought epic heroes were bullshit. He preferred the tragic clown. In the image in my head he is drinking a Guinness with a retsina chaser. We are drinking, laughing, yelling, fucking our way through Greece.

The second image is at Jim Morrison's grave, when the bust still had a head. A bottle of red wine, a baguette, a toast. A seemingly perfect moment between young drunk lovers until he spits out his bite of baguette, announcing that some bird shit had somehow gotten on the bread, and how hard we laughed in that moment. His laugh I mean. His laugh like no other laugh I ever heard in my life. His laugh like life itself. His laugh drawing laughter from all my sorrows. Mouth to mouth. Then it rained so hard the cobblestone paths sounded like they were applauding.

The third image is from Ireland, Doolin, where we scrambled down a cliffside embankment and lodged ourselves like oversized birds into the face of some craggy cliff wall at the lip of a strangely deep tidal pool. The tidal pool had dozens of sea anemones, submerged glow-in-the-dark greens and pinks, red and orange starfish, purple and black urchins. It was too cold to take our clothes off and get in the water. We took our clothes off and got in the water. I felt as close to a fairy-tale water creature as I'll ever get, I think. With the possible exception of how I feel now every time I face off from shore with a playful seal in the sea at the lip of the Pacific Ocean off the coast of Oregon. After we put our clothes back on, we drank Guinness in a pub and listened to Irish musicians playing jigs and reels most of the night.

I'm not surprised these images of love have a kind of fairy-tale or mythic feel to them. They remind me of how much I love storytelling. I am unable to stop writing stories. It would be true to say that there are pieces of Devin in everything I have ever written. Or true enough.

≈

THERE ARE also three images that fracture the frame of our love story, no matter how hard I try to forget them.

The night I came home late from work to a house with all the lights out in Eugene, Oregon. That night he walked across the living room in the dark until he met me at the door. He gently pointed a gun at my chest, resting the end of it on my sternum, and asked me to stop loving him, the smell of Jameson bigger than any vow. A Sig Sauer P365 Romeo.

The night I went dancing with a woman lover who tried to woo me away from Devin, how he came to the dance club and dragged me out by the arm, how my arm still carried the trace of his name where I'd carved it after a drunken argument, just as his arm carried my name, how my arm nearly broke when caught by my blue Toyota truck door, a blameless fracture, only a pain I still feel when it rains, only a trace of his name. I wore a vintage purple dress with tiny yellow roses embroidered all over it. The blue Toyota truck door shredded the sleeve.

The third image is one I never saw myself. I heard about it. Devin did time for setting his girlfriend's car on fire after she left him, after he left me for her. He wrote to me about it in the Book of Devin. I can see him pouring gasoline on the car. I can see him lighting a match—not a lighter—an actual match, the old-school wooden kind, which he described in detail. I can see the moment before he throws the match toward the car, two twin flames reflected in his dark eyes. I can see the car burst into flames. Or put slightly differently, I can see his heart burning from the inside out in the form of her burning car. How much hurt and longing. Like a child's want. *Please love me please just love me I'm falling to pieces I'm falling I'm leaping I'm falling.*

≈

It seems fitting that fragments are all I have left of Devin. The pieces are sediments of a sort. They can be arranged and rearranged endlessly to make new stories. If I am learning anything from his death, I am learning that.

And this: I can't think about Devin anymore without thinking about my mother, and not just because they are both dead, although I suspect that has some weight. The three great deaths that mark my life so far are my daughter Lily's, my mother Dorothy's, and Devin's. But that's not why I think of Devin and my mother together.

Devin and Dorothy are like a long slow drink from a bottle.

Devin and Dorothy were both alcoholics. They were both capable of extreme sadness and extreme jolts of joy. They may each have had undiagnosed mental health difficulties, though neither of them ever underwent specific medical testing. They both told me they loved me, and I wanted with all my heart to believe them, but I didn't know how to carry it, or even feel it.

When we look back at the past, how willing are we to face off with who we were in the storyline?

Devin fell for several other women while we were married.

Dorothy did not save me from my father's abuse.

I could not save my mother.

I could not save my daughter.

I could not save Devin.

So many sentences are hiding underneath other sentences.

I did not love my mother the way she wanted to be loved.

I loved my daughter who died the day she was born, and so that love lived in a death story.

I loved Devin the way my mother wanted to be loved. I confess, I adored him.

To save someone is a narrative trope.

Adoration is its own dangerous leap or fall.

≈

WHENEVER MY GRANDMOTHER PAULINE, my mother's mother, came up in conversation between us, my mother's entire face would go soft and slack, her blue eyes would pool up in their sockets, and before she could even say the sentence I could see that it was true that she adored her mother. The word "adoration" comes from the Latin *adōrātiō*, meaning to give homage, to venerate, to worship.

When my mother was dying of breast and lung cancer, when a great sorrow would come over her face, I could see that part of the sorrow was that no one in her life ever loved her the way that she loved her mother. Not even her mother.

I know that feeling.

No one has ever loved me the way that I loved Devin, either.

I now thank all the stars in the sky for that. I understand profoundly now how adoration leaves the giver eviscerated, eaten alive. And the weight of the adoration on the person who is adored could kill them.

How heavy the load of my adoration was. Impossible to carry forward, I imagine. Into any story. At the heart of my complete adoration of Devin was a kind of bleating, like a second heartbeat begging amplification: *Please love me please love me please love over the hole where my heart should be I couldn't figure out how to love my mother and she couldn't figure out how to love me and my daughter died my heart is a blast crater.*

But something like an evaporation is taking place in my life now. A lifting of the terrible weight. A transmography.

I currently live nestled within an Oregon forest where deciduous alders and Sitka spruce conifers intermingle. The alders have small flat green leaves that drop in the winter, when the trees go dormant. Their ash gray–white bark is covered with moss and lichen in winter and spring. Their stands make vertical patterns that comfort me when I walk through them. The trees look like they have eyes. Because they are deciduous, every year they go through a death process called abscission. They die and resurrect. Alder trees here generally live about fifty to sixty years.

In contrast, the Sitka spruce is a mighty, evergreen conifer with a scaly trunk and wild, octopus arms. The needles are a deep dark green and the cones are reddish brown. The trunk diameter of a Sitka can grow up to and beyond sixteen feet. The Sitkas around my house tower over us. They feel like sentries, though I understand they probably don't give a shit about puny humans. They are likely over two hundred feet tall, and may be as old as two hundred years. Like me, Sitkas love rainy climates.

When I walk through the alder and Sitka forests surrounding our house, I sometimes come across organic artifacts. Animal bones, feathers of eagles or stellar jays, barred owls, varied thrushes, and ravens. Of course, cougar, black bear, elk, deer, and coyote scat is everywhere. Occasionally I'll find human things discarded, cigarette or candy wrappers, a soda can, or shotgun shells left by deer and elk hunters. And beer bottles. Not many, but they stand out. The world I live in is not urban. I've seen more animals and birds living here on a single day than I've seen cumulatively in my entire life.

Once I found a brown Guinness bottle nestled in the grass, an especially unusual brand to find out here.

I remember it was December. December is the month my daughter died, a date that just flashes up in my body every year whether I want it to or not, the same date Devin and I married. Before my thoughts could catch up to my actions, I picked up the Guinness bottle and I smelled it; a trace of the faint acrid old dark beer smell lingered, or I thought it did. It didn't look or smell like the bottle had been there very long, but I can't be sure. I just stood there with the alders and Sitkas, holding the bottle, staring at it.

Then I closed my eyes and put the bottle to my lips and tipped it up. Not a drop left.

When my thoughts did come, they were Devin drinking Guinness every day and night of our lives together, Devin drinking Guinness and Jameson whiskey in Ireland, in England, in Scotland, in Eugene, Oregon. Rivers of Guinness. Oceans. Devin as fluid as a dream. I think I wanted him to love me more than he loved alcohol. Another child kind of want.

The more he drank, the more empty he became.

When I find trash or beer bottles out in the forest here, I bring them back home with me to recycle or throw in the garbage. So I brought that Guinness bottle home. But I couldn't put it in the recycling bin.

The truth is I watched the life force leave Devin's body a swig at a time, like a bottle of Guinness trying to drown itself. He almost seemed like a metaphor for the cosmic universe: something endlessly poured into him, something endlessly pouring out. Sometimes I still catch myself thinking, Was he there at all in our eleven years together? Was I? Were we something together? Was he filling himself up, or emptying himself out? Was I any part of what filled him? Or was it me that emptied him? Did pieces of me go with him, into him, or did I just float away from Devin?

What's the story?

I remember wishing idiotic things toward the end of our story like I wish he could just drink me. I remember wishing I was a bottle of Guinness so that he wouldn't have to think about what was happening to us, and I wouldn't have to feel how bad it hurt that we couldn't make it work. I never stopped loving Devin. I probably still love him. But the story of that love is dispersing, rearranging, shapeshifting. I am learning to lay his body down.

Loving a drinker is like loving a river always leaving you for the ocean.

I put a note in the Guinness bottle, capped it, and threw it out into the Pacific Ocean where I live now, where my daughter Lily's ashes swim.

The note read: We tried.

I could have written and set to water the same note to my mother.

≈

THE YEAR I FOUND the Guinness bottle in the woods, Andy and I also received a manila envelope from the State of California Marin County Health and Human Services. I was born in Marin County, so at first I thought the manila envelope was something about me. But inside the envelope was a letter asking us if we would speak with them about the possibility of fostering Devin's twelve-year-old son. His son's mother had been detained for reasons that are none of my business. It seems no one had been listed as next of kin, and I was the closest next best thing. An ex-wife who had been with Devin for eleven years.

Stories can change, rearrange at any moment.

I thought about Guinness bottles and Sitkas, alders, mushrooms. Yellow roses, river rocks. Construction cranes, sandhill cranes, great blue herons. Bukowski poetry lines and blue pickup trucks and Jim Morrison's grave. Photographs of people and places creating palimpsests. Memories, hues, rhythms, and returns. Monsters and mythic women emerging from fairy tales or films or history. Manila envelopes on kitchen tables. Hummingbirds.

I thought about my son.

I thought about Devin's son—a boy reaching for father but finding only sky.

≈

IT TOOK US less than twenty minutes to say yes, yes, we would help in any way that seemed useful. I wonder, did we think we could save someone in this story? In the end, Devin's son was reunited with his mother, a hopeful kind of story. When we were briefly in that story space where a boy who carried the trace of Devin might braid into our story, I did not think about all the things Devin did to me that hurt me in ways I've spent the rest of my life releasing into ocean, into forests, into writing. I did not think about Devin drinking, or his father drinking, or my mother drinking. I thought instead about all the phenomenal and complex paintings and drawings he created, or how we traveled, how he brought waves of laughter back into my life after the death of my daughter. I thought about the sound of his deep and low voice, how I used to bury my face in his long dark hair. The weirdly long length of his eyelashes, the depth of his desire to live near the edge of something dangerous and alive, how much I loved him, even as I had no idea what love was. How my love could not save him.

How in the end I had to save myself by swimming away from his falling.

How if Devin's son ever wanted to hear beautiful stories about his father, or see or keep some of his paintings or drawings, look at the shapes of his father's handwriting and poetry, touch the pages, or even hold a lock of his father's hair, smell it, close his eyes and picture Devin, then someone who is not the center of the story, but one who can help carry and give over pieces of the story, would be there in the wings.

L: Does it hurt terribly?

B: Not right now. They say the skin may burn or hurt later. And the fatigue just makes me want to sleep forever.

(SISTERS BOTH THINKING OF FAIRY TALES)

L: Do you ever think about Mother when we are doing this?

(SISTERS HOLDING HANDS DURING
BREAST CANCER RADIATION TREATMENTS)

B: Not really. I just remember her as sweet and sad. Mostly I think of the legions of other women at my back, and then I'm less afraid.

L: Sometimes I feel like it's my fault she died. Like I should have gone to Florida and taken care of her.

B: You did go to Florida.

L: But I didn't stay.

B: That wasn't your story. You had a just-born baby boy.

L: I love you. When this is over let's eat like twenty cheeseburgers.

B: I love you. That's a good place for this story to go.

(LAUGHTER BETWEEN SISTERS)

≈

Solaces

*B*ecome a new story. Become a new creature. Conjure the new myths, new shapes, new voices and bodies. There may be journeys, but not just journeys. There may be carryings, transitions, silences, liminal spaces, circles, repetitions, returns, figures of being and becoming in place of achieving actions and knowing.

≈

Some of us have deep relationships with books, films, music, dance, with animals and trees and rivers and oceans, with sky or space, with rocks or dirt; these interconnections are as important as human-to-human relationships. Some of us will let our humanness slide to the side of the story sometimes. Some of us will rewild our hearts. Do not mourn us when we pass. We fed something.

≈

You are neither a sinner nor a saint. Those are stories that preceded you like ornate traps, sparkling and decorated with high drama. Theology, pathology, psychology, philosophy are landlocked maps. Your desire, your erotic energy, belongs to you alone and may or may not have anything to do with sexuality, but may have quite a bit to do with creativity, imaginal goo, the cosmos, and your relationship to the everything; your internal erotics hook up with all existence.

≈

BEING, like imagination, is trans. It moves. Across. Beyond. Through. Change. Shapeshifting. Interbeing. Interspecies.

≈

THERE WILL COME times in your life when you know that you must do something, or that you cannot do something, with your whole body. Trust those moments.

≈

THE LOVE STORIES you enter are always living and dying, and in that motion the love stories carry something stunning, some treasure that you will make use of the rest of your life. Our broken hearts are what we give each other so that we may endure: shared sorrow is also the seed of joy.

≈

YOUR FAMILY OF ORIGIN is only one kind of origin. Your ancestors track back to trees, water, minerals, space, otherness.

≈

INHERITED TRAUMA is a story form always open to dissolving and re-forming as something else. Beautiful alchemies. Lifedeath cycles. Reach. Leap. Unfurl. Tendril. Reshape.

≈

YOU MAY HAVE to open yourself up to new definitions of words and stories, like love, like family, like belief, like being, like becoming, like death and life, by letting go of old definitions and stories; do not be afraid. The unmooring is a tender regeneration, not oblivion.

≈

YOU MAY HAVE to lay some bodies down; you do not need to carry every body forever. We take turns moving the burdens from body to body to dirt to water to sky. Sometimes people who have the bodies for carrying life forget that carrying life is not the only way to be in a body. We have to remind each other there are many ways to carry life, to share life, to transfer life, to let go. Ask the animals. Ask the trees. Ask water.

≈

YOU ARE NEVER the same person twice; your story is ever-being. You are constantly changing, and that is everything.

≈

YOUR "FIELDS OF POSSIBILITY" are everything; mine have been art and water. What are yours?

≈

YOU ARE NEITHER male nor female to the exclusion of either. A femascular exists inside us all, like an evolutionary creature waiting to find form. Or some other word you invent. We are on the cusp of regenerating ourselves. What shapes are emerging from

your body? What new words? What new stories? What new relationships? Look around you. Mercifully, there are others. New
lexicons are coming. New forms of being. Not all of them are human, which maybe was the point of existence.

Your existence is part of an existence much larger than your human identity and ego, your private pain and sorrow—the larger
story needs all of us and the sediments of our experiences for any of
us to go on. Unfix. Unfurl.

≈

CERTAIN MAGICAL PEOPLE you know in your life are constantly
showing you how to see yourself differently, how to stand in a different position to events and emotions in your own story. There are
so many hands held out to you. These people are almost never who
you expect. Look in liminal spaces, accidental fissures, and cracks:
they are windows. Look behind you, too. Your periphery is not
nothing.

≈

YOUR FAILURES and fears are portals. Step through.

≈

YOUR LABOR has value beyond the institutions and constructs you
inhabit.

≈

SYNCHRONICITY, repetition, ritual, poetry, storytelling, art, silence, stillness, dream, alchemy, divination, song, gesture, circu-

larity, and meditation are thrilling alternatives to causal, linear, and colonization thinking. They are also older than we are. They have been waiting for us.

≈

STORYTELLING CAN be anything we want it to be—for my own part I hope that storytelling is becoming plural, shapeshifting. My place in the story is not important. The storytelling motion is.

≈

YOU MAY HAVE to shapeshift yourself; everything around you is showing you how every breath of your life—storytelling is a potentiality—the natural world, and the animal and elemental worlds are endlessly performing the way. Entering storytelling differently can help us travel into the everything with forms and patterns corresponding to our embodiment. Death is not the end you dread, though you may encounter sorrow; death is just a turn in the story that is bigger than any one of us. Death is always becoming.

≈

I TAKE with me winged creatures, cranes and crows, great blue herons and eagles, ospreys and egrets, hummingbirds, falcons and hawks and owls. I take with me the whale and dolphin, the narwhal and octopus, all the fish in the sea, the axolotl, the seal. I carry a hundred hues of yellow, all the books of my life, photographs and films and rocks. An undine making S shapes around my life in endless patterns. Shapeshifter. Warrior. Artist. I make my returns and regenerations. Synchronicities form shapes, dissipate, re-form. My

alone is a state of being let loose from individualism, exceptional-
ism, the lure of recognition. My alone is vast as water and connects
with otherness. Where the thirst of knowledge once lived nests a
hummingbird who can breathe underwater. Where I have bloomed
let me decompose and generate another's growth.

≈

NOW YOUR TURN. Make a list.

Acknowledgments

I always feel compelled to thank the first tree I loved, the one I climbed up again and again to escape my father and family, the one I told my first secrets and stories to. Or water: Lake Washington, where I first learned to swim; Lake Chelan, where I first learned to fish; the Pacific Ocean; rain; all the swimming pools of my life. Or the good dirt, where I have buried so many treasures. Individual rocks, collections, rocks in rivers or at the lip of the sea. Animals who have inhabited my life, my house, my world, more kin than kin. But who would understand what I mean?

I also feel the pull to thank dead people, which seems not at all odd to me, since I consider death to be alive in our lives, and I think our lives show us how the dead and the living intermingle endlessly, not as binaries, but as pieces of an existence larger than puny humans, the cosmos my evidence.

Forgive me for my odd gratitude gestures. This book is born from returning to imaginal worlds, the realm of memory and dream, with and without living humans.

So thank you, trees and animals, rocks from everywhere in the world, and the night sky. We all know where my storytelling originates.

Thank you to Devin, to Dorothy, and to beautiful baby Lily. To others you are dead, but to me you are in the weave of the cosmos, from which all stories are spun.

Thank you, desire. Thank you, death. Thank you, art. Thank you, water. All water.

Of course, all books only come into being through acts of passionate collaboration. I mean my god, I am so grateful that art collaborations between humans still exist in my lifetime, that books are something you can still hold in your hands, pass to another person. My gratitude to the entire editing, design, and production teams at Riverhead Books, including the great and kind Jake Morrissey, Ariel So, Delia Taylor, Katie Hurley, Sheila Moody, Alicia Hyman, Lorie Young, Shehrbano Hasan, Claire Vacarro, Amanda Dewey, Helen Yentus, and Lauren Peters-Collaer. My gratitude as well to all librarians and booksellers on planet Earth.

My entire adult life has been about working alongside others in collaborative community. You could say this labor keeps my heart beating, not beaten. Thank you to Janice Lee, Domi Shoemaker, Daniel Elder, Katie Guinn, and Leigh Hopkins, the Corporeal Writing Squad. You are the rest of me.

Thank you to my agent and dear friend Rayhané Sanders, without whom I'd not know how to bridge to the world.

Thank you to Calvert Morgan, who when presented with my strange forms of storytelling never asked why, but instead asked *what if?*

Gratitude to every writer and artist I have ever met, living or dead. Solidarity in art and heart. We take turns. We keep going. As many times as it takes to keep the story lit.

Thank you to my sister Brigid, who helped pull me through the impossible and into the everything. May we echo each other's odd love songs like stubborn birds and fish who found themselves in human form for a while.

And as always, my heart belongs to Andy and Miles Mingo, both of whom help me keep the stories alive, through every leap and dive.